The Breaking Point:
A Full-Circle Journey

Living Life beyond All the Broken Pieces

Michelle Hannah

iUniverse, Inc.
Bloomington

The Breaking Point: A Full-Circle Journey
Living Life beyond All the Broken Pieces

iUniverse books may be ordered through booksellers or by contacting:

iUniverse
1663 Liberty Drive
Bloomington, IN 47403
www.iuniverse.com
1-800-Authors (1-800-288-4677)

Because of the dynamic nature of the Internet, any web addresses or links contained in this book may have changed since publication and may no longer be valid. The views expressed in this work are solely those of the author and do not necessarily reflect the views of the publisher, and the publisher hereby disclaims any responsibility for them.

Any people depicted in stock imagery provided by Thinkstock are models, and such images are being used for illustrative purposes only.

Certain stock imagery © Thinkstock.

ISBN: 978-1-4697-7705-4 (sc)
ISBN: 978-1-4697-7706-1 (hc)
ISBN: 978-1-4697-7707-8 (e)

Library of Congress Control Number: 2012903057

Printed in the United States of America

iUniverse rev. date: 3/22/2012

Contents

Acknowledgments

To my daughter, Kyler, who has always been the first love of my life: I wrote this book to show you that all things are possible and that, no matter what you go through in life, I am always here—through the breakups, breakdowns, breakthroughs, and breakouts. My life experience is the evidence of the love that I have for you and of the fact that it reaches your past, present, and future.

To my parents, Tunk K. Hannah and Clarissa Hannah: Without you both there would be no Michelle R. Hannah. Because of your union, the journey that resulted in this book was possible, and for that I offer my deepest gratitude and love.

To my sister, Tina: The gratitude I have just cannot be expressed in words. The friendship and sisterhood you have shown are those of a true friend who sticks closer than a brother. Your friendship is evidence that blood does not have to intertwine us to make us deeply connected. God truly connected us, and when he did it, he did it right!

To Von, a true supporter: The inspiration and motivation to write this book came from a consistent push from one of the most inspiring individuals I have ever met: you. If it hadn't been for your constant push to write this book, even when I was at my lowest point, I don't know if I would have been able to write with courage and grace. In spite of it all, you encouraged me to always dream bigger.

To my uncle, Steve, the greatest uncle a girl could ask for: You have shown me the true definition of "for better or for worse, in sickness and in health."

When I thought I couldn't put one more foot in front of the other, you carried me until I could do it on my own.

To my spiritual sister Pastor Rhonda, who has challenged me to be the best me: I thank you. You were what I needed to get through the most diffi cult time in my life. The prayers and long conversations got me through the storms that were hitting literally moment to moment. You personify true friendship.

To my supporters, K. Curtis, K. Edwards, C. J. Gross, B. Hollaway ,T. Wright, T. Spaulding M. Tlapa and L.Thompson: You have held me accountable for living in the moment, and each of you have motivated me in a special way that will be embedded in my heart for a lifetime!

My Team Kawai Matthews, Rokael Lamaste, Ashley Sean Thomas, Michael Melendy, Amadu Turay and Dionne Phillips: You all made the transformation complete. Every word, chapter, and ultimately, every past journey came together on the day that my life met your expertise. As a result, magic happened!

To my friend of 30 years JH: Forgiveness is a choice but there is freedom in Letting Go and Letting God…Through the process of forgiveness, you can rise above and breakthrough the betrayal and pain. I had to and I did. I thank you for four months of proof that transformation can happen to anyone that is ready. Staying transformed is the real work. In your famous words "Just Do It."

In loving memory of my personal assistant, Loriana: "No mountain high enough, no river wide enough—not even death can separate us."

Introduction

You have had it! You have reached the *breaking point*. You know it because your physical, mental, or emotional strength has given away under stress. The situation is now critical. You finally acknowledge the issue, and you are motivated to face it. Ah, but then the *breakdown* follows. This is the time when you are working on yourself. Once you start the work, you can expect pain and fear. You will feel as though you want to quit, and you will make up excuses for why completing the journey isn't as important as it was when you first acknowledged your breaking point. You have to make the choice whether to face your fear or run away once again. If you choose to face the fear, you will continue on your personal journey, and if you decide to run away, you will fail the test again.

As you push through the work, you will find that self-reflection, forgiveness, and healing are essential. Depression usually sets in at some point during the breakdown, but you must push through the darkest hole and embrace the light. When the light hits, you want to finally *break it*—whatever *it* is! Your *breakthrough* is now here. You can glimpse the results of the work you put in, and you are confident and hopeful. The tests are coming one by one, because it's now time to see if you have learned the right lessons. You are now equipped to tackle the tests and ultimately pass them. You know what transformation looks and feels like. You adore the true you.

Finally you have arrived at the moment you have been awaiting, and that is *breakout*. The burden has been lifted, and you are living your purpose. It's no longer about what you can get; it's about what you can give. You are living in each moment, and you know that tomorrow will take care of itself. By doing what you love to do and living in the moment, you will live beyond all the *broken pieces*. All the phases—*breakup, breakdown, breakthrough,* and *breakout*—make up your *full-circle journey*.

Chapter 1

Breakups

In our lifetimes, we break many things. Some we are attached to, and some we are not. When we break something that we are attached to, we feel the need to mend it. Have you ever broken something that had sentimental value and felt the same anxiety that accompanies the breakup of a relationship? You immediately try to find something that will put the object back together. Anything will do: superglue, tape, or—from a relationship point of view—change might mend things. The thought behind this frenzy is that you just don't want to let go of the valuable item. On the other hand, if you break something that has no value to you, you quickly toss it in the trash can with no thought or emotional attachment.

This chapter will take you on a journey through reason, seasonal, lifetime, self, and spiritual breakups. It will define these breakups and assist you in overcoming their challenges.

The Reason Breakup

In my life, I have found that there are five categories of relationship breakups. The first category is the breakup that occurs because of a reason. When a reason breakup occurs, it is because the individual in your life is there to meet a need that you have expressed outwardly or inwardly. This relationship usually assists you through a difficulty; provides you with guidance and support; or aids you physically, emotionally, or spiritually on your journey. This relationship might seem like a godsend to you, and it is.

Without any wrongdoing on your part—and usually at an inconvenient time—the person might say or do something to bring the relationship to an abrupt end. Sometimes the individual walks away or passes away. Maybe he or she does something that is so hurtful or character damaging that you have to walk away. The bright side is that your need has been met and your desire has been fulfilled.

When I relocated back to California, I felt forced to rekindle several relationships after a longtime friend decided to make my health issues very public among some childhood friends. I am a very private person, and I had no interest in rekindling relationships from my past, especially as a result of something so personal. I tried to give this friend the benefit of the doubt. Perhaps it was to generate support, or maybe disclosing personal information was just this individual's way. At this point, I had no choice but to face people when they began to confront me with the information that they had been given. I allowed people back into my life for the sake of support. It was a bittersweet experience. Very few of the rekindled relationships ended up being permanent; most of them were only there for a reason. My anger and disappointment about the disclosure of my personal business began to lessen when I realized that my reconnection to those people had happened for a compelling reason, whether it felt good or bad.

One relationship I had fulfilled a need for a family weekend. A friend literally flew in for a weekend and introduced me to her large family. She made me feel very loved for those couple of days and showed me the importance of family support. I felt that I couldn't have made it through that time's particular storm if she had not been there. Then, without any reason that made sense to me, the relationship dwindled quickly.

Another example is a working relationship that turned into a brief friendship. I had learned to depend on this relationship for several reasons. To this day, I don't think the person involved knew that I trusted her immensely. We would have such a great time when we went out. Her youthful spirit reminded me of when I was her age, and it made the reality of my health struggles easier. I allowed her to become very close to my business, and it seemed as though she were a godsend because of all the help she gave on various projects and the enlightenment that she provided on detailed issues. Thinking back over it, she *was* a godsend. God sent her for many reasons but specifically to facilitate a project that saved some cancer patients' lives and enhanced quality of life for many survivors. Many times when I was very ill, she came and sat by my side.

During this time in my life, I needed that extra push that she gave, and the relationship fulfilled me. Without any warning, however, she hurt me in a way that brought the relationship to an abrupt end. At first I was very hurt, and I thought, *How can she believe something that is so character damaging without truly finding out the facts?* Nevertheless, I was able to let go, to move on, to feel a genuine love for what she had brought to my life, and to hope that I had brought the same gift to hers.

Sometimes we do not know the reason for a relationship—or a breakup— until months or even years later. For example, I once fell down the stairs in my building and fractured three bones in my foot. I didn't know how major the fractures were until I was still in the boot three months later. My foot, neck, and shoulder were in distress. I began physical therapy, and the therapist stated that I needed to stretch. Had I been stretching regularly, the therapist claimed, my muscles never would have become so compacted.

At that moment I realized the reason for a past relationship. Not knowing the reason for that relationship had troubled me for years. Now I realized the reason: that person had advised me about my health. He often told me how important it was for me to exercise and to stretch. He had even said that there would come a time in life when I would wish I had stretched. He gave me specific directions regarding my diet, but I refused to listen. I told myself that he was communicating in a destructive way and that he should just love me for me. Part of that was true—he could have expressed his advice differently—but the bottom line is that he was right. I believe he was showing that he cared enough about my life to tell me the truth. We were never supposed to be involved in a *seasonal* relationship, only a *reason* relationship that met the need of the moment—and that need was focusing on my health. Had I done that, I wouldn't still be struggling with my diet and health today.

That relationship happened almost ten years ago. In order to wake up, I had to hear the words of my physical therapist, who told me I needed to stretch, and my doctor, who said that I was slowly killing myself with a poor diet. Back in the time of my relationship, I hadn't been overweight, so in response to my friend's advice, I had thought, *Who is he to suggest I change my diet?* I'd assumed his criticism was about my physical appearance when it was really about what was going on *inside* my body. Ten years later I finally figured out the reason for that relationship: a friend was trying to save and enhance my life. I just couldn't see it in a positive light because I'd been so blinded by all the negative aspects of our relationship. Today I believe that a bad diet can be the source of a deadly illness and that a good diet is the key to good health.

When we attempt to upgrade a reason relationship into a season relationship or a lifetime relationship, we do ourselves a disservice. If I had just accepted the positive reason for my relationship with my friend, I would have avoided all the pain and grudges that came along with that relationship. Again, we don't always know the reason for a reason breakup, but when we continue to try to force something that isn't working, it could be that we are trying to force the relationship to be what we want it to be instead of what it should be.

During some of my hardest days in California, many of my relationships consisted of encouraging e-mails, text messages, beautiful voice mails, and occasional visits. These short-lived relationships showed me that people can have every intention to be there in the manner they promised, but they can't follow through because they are there for a limited reason. On the days when I didn't think I would make it or needed help to make it, these relationships fulfilled their purposes. I wanted them to be there for the long haul and was disappointed when they weren't, but now I realize that they did what they were supposed to do.

Recap:

Characteristics	Lessons
The relationship meets a need that you have expressed outwardly or inwardly.	Do not attempt to make a *reason* breakup into a *seasonal* breakup.
The need and desire of the *reason* relationship are met.	When it's time for the relationship to end, move on!
The person assists you through a difficulty, provides you with guidance and support, or helps you physically, emotionally, or spiritually.	Without any wrongdoing, the relationship comes to an end.

The Seasonal Breakup

A seasonal breakup is the end of a relationship that is in your life for a season. This relationship is there to help you grow and learn. It may teach you to do something that you have never done or always wanted to do but didn't because of fear. This relationship gives you so much joy that you can't imagine living without it. You feel that this relationship will be a lifetime experience—but once the season is over, the relationship is over. You haven't done anything wrong; it's just that the season has changed, and it's time to move on. But if you are determined to hold on to the relationship once it has run its course, the consequences are often disappointment and hurt.

We generally think of family relationships as lifetime experiences, but sometimes they do not fit certain parts of our journeys. Family is always going to be family, by title, but you do not need to keep unhealthy

was over. The good news is that if I hadn't been fired from that position, I would not have ended up in the education industry, and I would not have become the first African American woman to become an assistant dean at a well-respected university. This seasonal working relationship fulfilled me and gave me great joy. I wanted it to be a lifetime experience because it gave me confidence, hope, and a sense of stability. But it was time to move on, and although I didn't want to, I was forced to. In the end, it hurts less when you don't fight against the season's end. Welcome spring after winter, and enjoy the smells of the flowers.

Recap:

Characteristics	Lessons
Seasonal breakups are in your life for a season.	They teach you something you haven't done or have always wanted to do.
They give you an opportunity to learn and to grow.	Know and accept when your season has changed.
They can apply to personal or professional relationships.	Know that once the season is over the relationship is over.
They have the appearance of lifetime relationships.	Don't etch this person in your lifelong process.

The Lifetime Breakup

The lifetime breakup is the ending of a relationship that you can never revisit. It's the breakup that takes time, for you must heal and come to understand all the lessons that you learned from the relationship. Lifetime breakups usually happen with people you love or have a strong emotional attachment to. Time and time again it's the relationship that you can't seem to let go of. You know you need to walk away—or even run away—but you stay. It is the relationship that causes you to hit rock bottom, to tolerate another person's unacceptable behavior, and to lose your self-esteem. This relationship gets to the core of who you really are compared to who you want to be. It breaks down that false representation that you show on that first date or for that first year. Sometimes in the course of the relationship you are broken down into many pieces and are forced to look at yourself in the mirror and make a change. The best way to handle this type of breakup is to apply the life lessons you learn to future relationships.

I took wedding vows that stated, "To have and to hold, from this day forward, for better or for worse, for richer or for poorer, in sickness and in health, to love and to cherish till death do us part. And hereto I pledge you my faithfulness." What intimate vows these are. Did I mean them? Absolutely not—and it wasn't until my health was failing that I understood these vows and their importance. I can't be sure of my ex-husbands' actions, but eleven years after my most recent divorce, I can say that I now take these vows seriously. I have studied them, and I realize that I wasn't ready to be committed back then. I openly apologize to my exes for making a mockery of the commitment. I wasn't ready then—not even 5 percent—but as of today, I am 100 percent respectful of the meaning of these vows, and if I am ever blessed to be in the position to state these vows and to receive them again, it *will* be till death do us part.

My divorces were lifetime breakups. Lifetime breakups are the most difficult because these are the relationships that you cannot revisit. Once they're over, they are *over*. You may ask, "What about people who remarry the same person after divorce? Should they not have revisited those relationships?" My answer is that once you have divorced in your heart and you know that the relationship was killing your spirit, stealing your dreams, and failing to enhance your life in any way, you must leave it alone, let it go, and don't revisit it!

I have learned the biggest lessons about myself and about life through relationships that I thought would last a lifetime. Here are the main lessons:

- Love isn't negative.

- Honesty is critical.

- Relationships don't define me.

- Not every serious relationship is a lifetime relationship.

- Marriage is hard work.

- I should always trust my first instinct.

What if I could have learned these lessons just by dating and then having a healthy reason or seasonal breakup? Did I really have to turn these relationships into lifetime breakups? Did I need the drama in my life? In retrospect, I think I could have done many things differently, but I made the same mistake in judgment more than once—and for some of the same reasons. Those reasons were the need to be loved, the need to be taken care of financially and emotionally, the need to be happy, and the need to drown out my pain by hiding within something or someone else. For these reasons, I made an active decision not to walk away, run away, or sprint away. But before I become filled with regret, I remember that my lifetime breakups taught me essential lessons that will aid in the success of my future relationships.

The pain and the unforgivingness—of yourself and the other—are the most difficult trials to overcome with lifetime breakups. These breakups really get to the foundation of who you are, and at times that is most painful—because the mirror is your truth. Forgiveness is not for the other person; it's for *you*. It is your personal gift to yourself. Forgiveness is your reward for overcoming the tragedy and the abysmal situations that you have just experienced. Don't be fooled; this is the hardest thing for most people to overcome, because often they think forgiveness means forgetting. Forgiveness means to release and let go. It is a choice and a commitment to live in the present and let go of the past. True forgiveness will give you peace that will help you go on with your life.

As for the people who walk away from us, please *let them walk*! If you chase after them, it will only hurt you more and prolong the pain. You cannot talk someone into staying with you, being faithful to you, showing up to make sure you are all right, or loving you. How can you knowingly tie your purpose to anybody who has left you or who wants to leave you? Know this: everyone who was not tied to my purpose has left me—or I have left him. The more I fought to keep him close or tried to prevent embarrassment the worse the situation became. If a relationship takes your joy, peace, and sanity, then break it up, break it off, and break away. Once you get this in your soul, you will understand the breakup and the breakdown that have to occur, the breakthrough that will follow, and the breakout that will enable you to live your best life!

Although you can never revisit a lifetime relationship, if you should cross your ex's path, you can hold your head up high and smile, knowing that courage is an innate quality and you are feeling nothing but peace and joy. In that moment, if the person asks how you have been, let your reply be, "I am happy." Hold no grudge, no resentment, and no pain; instead, feel only peace and happiness.

Recap:

Characteristics	Lessons
Lifetime breakups can never be revisited.	The experience will aid in the success of future relationships.
You are forced to make a change.	When people walk away from you, let them walk.

The Self-Breakup

To me, the ultimate breakup is the breakup with yourself. When you break up with yourself, it can be positive or negative. It's *negative* when you break away from who you really are and pretend that you are someone else, for the sake of acceptance. It's *positive* when you break up with the person you are right now to become the person you need to be. That only happens through growth, true reflection, pain, and mistakes.

The reasons that are usually connected to a relationship breakup are the same reasons that exist when you begin to break away from yourself. You may no longer trust your own judgment, and your communication with yourself has become nonexistent. Lying and cheating are the most common reasons why two people break up. Isn't being afraid of the truth lying to yourself? Isn't it cheating and taking the easy way out when you don't make the effort to do the work on yourself? Your self-esteem affects the health of all your relationships. If need is the major emphasis, the relationship can't be healthy. On the other hand, positive self-esteem can greatly enhance a relationship.

Over the years, I noticed that I battled with low self-esteem. I lied to myself and could not trust myself. I was lost in the facade of who I was versus who I was portraying myself to be. I was full of pride and unable to forgive myself. The result was a much-needed breakup with me—meaning who I was at that time. Like any breakup, it hurt, and it was not easy to walk down that self-reflection road to get to a state of health and happiness.

I told myself that I was in control, and I was convinced that I was completely unselfish. It's painful to admit, but 50 percent of the reason that I gave so much is that I wanted back what I gave. I wanted someone to heal my pain. I felt that I deserved love because of my deep pain, not because of my courage.

When you battle with low self-esteem, you feel unworthy, and in my opinion, feeling unworthy is the common denominator of all pain. I felt that if I treated all other people as if they were good enough, maybe they would treat me as if I were good enough. I would give and give—but eventually I would feel empty, because I seldom received what I needed. I often took my last bit of energy to make someone else happy. There were two reasons for this: I loved seeing people smile, and I wanted to feel worthy and, ultimately, loved. Well, the truth is, the moment you realize your self-worth, everything you give becomes truly sincere—you no longer require getting something back. You give love to yourself, first and foremost, and the result is healing. Through my own healing, I realized that the definition of self-worth was Michelle Hannah.

I will never regret my journey to define who I was and the freedom that I longed for. The courage that it took to do this was life-defining for me. There were many tears and many lonely moments.

It's hard to face yourself and not blame anyone else for the position you are in. Other people might contribute to your pain, but the choice is always yours. No one can force you to be or not be something. No one can take your freedom away unless you allow them to. Of course, you must abide by certain laws, but in the privacy of your own home and your own mind you can be free. I can dance naked and pretend I can sing like Jill Scott around my house without worrying about being arrested. And, in my mind, I can be anywhere and feel uninhibited. Trust me, there are many times when I am dancing around in my head, free as a bird, birthday suit and all!

Recap:

Characteristics	Lessons
It is negative when you break away from who you really are and pretend that you are someone else, for the sake of acceptance.	Your soul is opened and helps you embrace new perspectives.
It is positive when you break away from your current self to become your better self.	You are challenged to make new discoveries.
It is needed when you don't know your self-worth.	You learn not to be fearful of change and to be ambitious emotionally, romantically, intellectually, creatively, and spiritually.

The Spiritual Breakup

Spiritual breakups are the best, but sometimes they feel the worst. The best thing about spiritual breakups is that your soul opens up and embraces new perspectives through a variety of different religious teachings. The worst thing about spiritual breakups is that what you have believed to be true all your life is now in question, and you are challenged to have the courage to explore your new discoveries.

My spiritual connection is God, and it took a spiritual breakup to get me to the breaking point that moved me to the next phase, which I will discuss in detail in the next chapter. I was brought up in the church. My mother told me thatI was put on the altar at six months for a type of christening that meant my life was dedicated to God. Looking back, I remember that I was always in church, but I do not remember having an intimate relationship with God. It was more of a relationship with the church and its rules. There were so many rules that consisted of what you couldn't do. The few things that you could do as a Christian consisted of marriage and church events. It wasn't until years later that I realized that this line of strict religious teaching was more about control and less about spirituality, intimacy, and understanding the word of God.

I grew up in a Pentecostal church and was often amused by the charismatic shouts and dancing that took place at every service. I was confused by the many personal interpretations of the scriptures in the Bible. I felt as though God wasn't all love but could actually be very mean; God picked and chose whom he loved. What I mean by this is that the saints (Christians in the church) would treat as unworthy anyone who wasn't dressed properly, who spoke out of turn, who had a suspect past, or who wasn't the picture-perfect Christian. I asked myself, *Isn't the church for everybody—the prostitute, the drug addict, the mentally and physically sick, the brokenhearted, the suicidal, the abandoned, the liar, and all who could be considered unlovable?* I attended private schools up until high school. Although they were either Catholic or Christian schools, I still felt this discrimination by Christians who seemed to want to pick and choose those whom God loved.

I was a childhood actress, so I experienced plenty of rejection. I felt I was never good enough, even when I landed a part in a movie or commercial. I thought that the church should be an escape from the rejection, but I was taught that the church had a right to be discriminating, and so did God. This way of teaching was different from what I felt and read in the Bible. The God I knew from the Bible was all-loving, and he loved unconditionally.

At the young age of eighteen, I thought that in order to be what they called "saved," all you could do was get married and attend church events. I was told that I was a sinner by wanting to experience things like traveling, going to a wine-tasting, watching certain programs on TV, enjoying sex within marriage, roller-skating, dancing, dating more than one person before marrying, dating without a chaperone, going to a therapist, wearing makeup, or even wearing pants. So what did my friends and I do? We got married at young ages and divorced at young ages.

I cannot express the pain of my first marriage and divorce. Being so young, I lacked knowledge of how to have a real, healthy relationship. How could I have freedom in marriage when I had no freedom as an individual? I lived in constant fear of the church. I didn't realize until almost twenty years later that I had been missing intimacy at a spiritual level. How could I expect intimacy in my relationships when I didn't know it within myself?

This series of events led me to break up with the church. I still believed in and revered God. What I was really breaking away from was the rigid rules of the church, which did not lead me down my own path to God. God wanted me to be free to love and to be loved. I was on a journey to find what I truly believed about who God was to me, the definition of true intimacy and love in a relationship, and the meaning of spiritual freedom.

This was a long journey, and I met many people from different cultures, walks of life, and spiritual backgrounds. I learned not to be judgmental and to embrace some form of peace and serenity from each religion that

I studied. I had been taught that all religions besides Christianity were wrong and that I would go to hell if I studied or read anything besides the Bible. Well, when I studied parts of Hinduism, I found that certain beliefs were very similar to Christian ones. Both Hinduism and Christianity contain a divine commandment of perfect righteousness and hold that we are accountable for our actions. They also share a strong focus on unselfishness, perfect mental peace, and detachment from worldly desires. By becoming aware of these commonalities, I realized that if people would just not judge others and would be open to learning and growing, they might find that they are more similar than different. Through the Celebrate Life Foundation, which I started in 2004, I applied the true meaning of perfect unselfishness and knowledge of self. I am still working toward perfect mental peace.

In 2009, I studied Buddhism for a short period of time. Again, I found that Christianity and this alternative religion had some common principles. Humility, meekness, and meditating on what is positive and good are essential to being either an observant Christian or an observant Buddhist. Again I realized that a religion that I had been taught was evil and completely the opposite of what was righteous had some similarities to my own. I found that the Buddhists I met were some of the most centered and humble people I had ever come across. They were all about getting rid of the *drama*!

In 2009 I moved back to California, which ended up being the worst move I had ever made. My life seemed to be unraveling quickly. I was the unhappiest that I had ever been since my dad had died. I was missing Washington DC, which I had considered home for the past six years. I missed the culture and the museums. I missed the many lounges, where I had spent timeless hours networking and speaking about investments and life. Once I had embraced some of the teachings of Buddhism— meditation, freedom, speaking the truth, acting in a nonhurtful way, and seeking wisdom that purifies the mind—my spiritual journey had expanded. The Washington Monument in DC has beautiful flags surrounding it, as well as many beautiful personal memories. This was where I had learned how to meditate and to experience true freedom.

Once I moved to California, I didn't have that place. I tried to put a flag up and duplicate that feeling of peace, but it wasn't the same. I had to realize that it was not the flag but the inner peace that I was striving and hungering for.

Recap:

Characteristics	Lessons
The need for peace, specifically spiritual peace	God is not in constant judgment of you, but other people are.
The need for intimacy with God and the courage to take your spiritual journey	Open your heart to intimacy, and you can open your heart to having an intimate relationship with God.

Breakup to Breakdown

In 2010, my life broke up into many pieces, and I had no clue how to recover. Many of my close relationships broke up. My mother and I had a very hurtful breakup that cut deeper than any previous separation. A close relationship of twenty-seven years ended, and the betrayal that I felt tore at me as if my insides had disintegrated. A very good friend passed away, which left me in a very confusing place. Many people with whom I had reconnected for a very short time were separating from my life at a very rapid pace (reason breakups); on the other hand, some of those reconnected relationships ended up being a part of my full-circle journey. I was suffering from both an illness and several false accusations. These accusations were assassinating my character, which was sacred to me. After all, I had built my whole life around my character; I felt that my word and my life should speak for themselves. I had worked hard to build a labor of love—my foundation—and it seemed that it was all about to be destroyed in a matter of one day.

I didn't realize it at the time, but my life had begun to spiral out of control. After several incidents, one last blow pushed me over the edge. That over-the-edge experience was a nervous breakdown—yes, a *breakdown*. The gossip, the voice mails, the e-mails, the lies, the truths, the betrayals, the breakups, the physical and mental pain, the vulnerability, the bad move to California, the money and contracts lost—all these thoughts were racing through my mind every hour on the hour.

Through therapy, a close-knit support team, true forgiveness, a struggle with the issue of abandonment, and major tears, I came full circle to the most important thing that I had broken away from—God. This time around, I discovered who God was and what he represented in my life. He definitely wasn't discriminating, mean, or anything but all-loving. Even at a time when I was considered unlovable and had hit the definition of rock bottom, he loved me through it all. When all others had failed me and turned their backs on me, he was there. The betrayal I felt was so deep that my breakdown literally knocked me to my knees. It wasn't until I was on my back that I called out to God, just as you would call out to your daddy for help. You see, Christianity was the third religion I studied after my spiritual breakup, and it felt most comfortable for my lifelong journey. Luckily, I realized that I didn't have to reject the attributes that I had taken from other religions.

I have learned that three life circumstances inevitably result in a breakup: sickness, incarceration, and financial ruin. In life, it is so important to be confident that the people you keep in your close circle are tied to your destiny. If they are not, they will not be there for the long haul, especially if you find yourself in one of those three circumstances. In fact, when you master the four phases—breakup, breakthrough, breakdown, and breakout—you will find yourself staying away from anyone or anything that is not tied to your destiny. That way, you will avoid the anger, pain, and disappointment that result when people let you down.

For instance, when you are going through a life-threatening illness, it is particularly hard for people to be consistent—and it's darn near impossible if they don't truly love you. After a couple of months, people who are not tied to your destiny or journey will walk away. They may intend to be there, but they can't provide you with what you need or what they have promised. If this happens, don't take it personally, and please don't carry the pain. If you do, you will postpone both the journey and the lesson.

If you get arrested, trust me, you will know who loves you and who your true friends are. I have been in some very difficult situations, in which I have seen dear friends arrested because of white-collar crime, and I have been accused because of association. I have also been in a situation in which I was falsely accused. The lesson I learned is that when you have a breakdown in reality, your objectivity or lack of control can determine your decisions.

According to our justice system, you are innocent until proven guilty. However, sometimes you are proven guilty in the eyes of the courts even though you are truly innocent. If you are arrested, take note of who comes to bail you out. Notice who arrives to give his car title as collateral to get you out of a situation with no questions asked, just pure love and support. For certain, this individual is a friend. On the other hand, if no one shows up, please don't be angry. I know it's hard not to feel alone, but someone will support you, no matter what, and that is God.

When I realized this, my relationship with God finally made sense. I understood that he loves me unconditionally. He forgives me for any sin right after I commit it. I may have broken up with him, but only for a season, and I know he didn't let go through summer, fall, winter, or spring. The relationship with God is the only relationship that withstands any kind of breakup—reason, seasonal, lifetime, self, and spiritual. It doesn't matter if you break up with him; he will never break up with you. He is always there. My spiritual journey led me to a huge "aha" moment: love covers a multitude of sin and hurts, and mine is an all-season God. As a result of my journey, I learned that this power loved me so much that even though someone was assassinating my character, he still stood by. I needed a major miracle in my mind and body, and something deep within told me that this power would see me through—and that it had been seeing me through the entire time on my full-circle journey.

Recap:

Breakdown defined	Lessons
Over the edge	True love is all-powerful.
Separation	Know the meaning of your own relationship with God.
Character assassination	Do not judge, or you will be judged.
Physical and mental pain	A breakdown in reality; your objectivity and lack of control can determine your decision making.

Chapter 2

Break Down—Not Me

When it comes to the breakdown phase, the word *humility* comes to my mind. This is the most humble place that you will ever be. At some point in life you will experience a breakdown that will lead you either to destruct or to restrict your life. But when you choose to face the issues, be prepared for the fallout. That fallout could be your darkest hour.

According to my doctors, I had a nervous breakdown—but it was a breakdown in every area of my life. During this time, I thought about many things, but one thing that stood out was the life of Abraham Lincoln. Before he became president, he experienced thirty years of defeat and failure—including a nervous breakdown after the loss of his fiancée. The death of his beloved was the final straw that broke down his total spirit. He was so broken that he stayed in bed for six months. I didn't become bedridden, but my mind felt as if it were in the same depression and prison that Abe had once been in. I checked out of what I knew as my workaholic and cushy life to finally take care of *me* for six months. Given the odds stacked against me and the back-to-back failures and traumas, my life seemed to parallel Abraham Lincoln's.

What is a breakdown? It is a sudden lapse in health and strength that causes you to cease functioning. Your purposes, occupation, close and distant relationships, physical health, and mental health come to an abrupt standstill. When it comes to the breakdown phase, the word *humility* comes to my mind. This is the most humble place that you will ever be. In this phase, you are up close and personal with an overwhelming feeling of embarrassment. You face the necessity of being honest with yourself, no matter how difficult it may be. You can no longer run from honesty, because lying is no longer an option. When you truly are in the breakdown phase, you feel a sense of loneliness, but at the same time you welcome isolation. This place of brokenness is also one of confusion. You're humble and open to another direction, even if it's quite different from any path that you have ever taken. You are ready to look at yourself in the mirror and become strong enough to face what's staring back. The Michael Jackson song "Man in the Mirror" illustrates the point of breakdown—specifically the line that says it's time to make a *change*. Clearly, an adjustment needs to be made.

Recap:

- A breakdown is a sudden lapse in health and strength that causes you to cease functioning.

- You feel a sense of loneliness, but at the same time you welcome isolation.

- It's the most humble and honest place that you will ever be.

- Abraham Lincoln had a nervous breakdown, suffered from depression, and became president of the United States of America.

It's Time to Restructure

Speaking of adjustment, during my breakdown phase I was diagnosed with adjustment disorder, a psychogenic fugue episode, and post-traumatic stress disorder. I temporarily experienced amnesia, insomnia, depression, panic attacks, major anxiety, dissociation from reality, suicidal thoughts, and paranoia. Was I crazy? Of course not—I had just reached a breaking point with reality. I had allowed anxiety and fear to overtake me, and I couldn't find my way back on track. While previously I had been able to function despite pain and stress, this time I had reached the point of breaking.

Aside from when my daddy died, this was the darkest time in my life. It hurt more than anything I had been through. Not only was I physically ill, but my mental state was now compromised. I could barely focus on anything. It didn't help that people were making some very harsh claims, some that I could understand and some that were blatant lies. The lies were about my character and circumstances that people thought were the gospel. I tried to understand how people I had known for more than half my life could state things that they knew would hurt me immensely and possibly put my professional character in major question.

The truth is that I finally had faced the truth about my past and present, and I was scared about my future. A long list of events and situations hit me all at once. I couldn't stop them; they just kept coming. It's amazing: before you have a breakdown, the truth hits you full force. The only lies left are that you can't handle the truth and that there is no way out. The details of what I was going through are not important, but I feel comfortable sharing the overall circumstances that sent me into a breakdown:

- Failed marriages
- Physically abusive relationships
- Attempted molestation
- Dad's death
- Several health issues that were not improving
- The stress of juggling a career, single parenthood, running a foundation, and dealing with the consistent death of cancer patients
- Pressure to be perfect in many areas and for many people—specifically, for my mother—when I was far from it
- The guilt of furthering my career that, although it created a financially stable environment for my daughter, took away quality mother-daughter time
- Secrets that I had kept to protect others, which had nearly killed my spirit

In response to my adjustment disorder and post-traumatic stress disorder, my therapist made a profound statement: "You need to restructure your life." I strongly related to the word *restructure,* and I knew that if I could just hold on to the meaning of that statement, my life would never be the same. I was slowly but surely becoming confident that I had a chance at happiness and healthy relationships. At times during this process I felt like a newborn baby because I was simply open to the right direction and the right path for my life. I no longer had the strength to resist. The unhealthy part of me was just surviving, not living. It was slowly dying—boy, was it a painful death—but the new life that was in the distant future was coming closer every day.

Many nights I lay awake, or I would wake up at two, four, or six o'clock in the morning. I didn't know what it was like to sleep through the night. I had a thousand racing thoughts, and my mind couldn't analyze them or filter them quickly enough. Sometimes I would feel impulsive. At two in the morning I'd feel this enormous urge to escape to a place where no one knew me, to make a fresh start. I just wanted to get away, to start all over and escape the pain that ran deeper than the darkest hole you can imagine. I felt out of control, and I could no longer organize simple tasks.

Being physically ill, and being misdiagnosed repeatedly, made me feel that I was running out of time, yet there were so many things that I hadn't done. I wanted a second chance, and I wanted to finally *live* this time around. I wanted to have no regrets—just excitement, joy, and a love such as I had never known. I wanted to sing with the same passion as Jill Scott, Patti LaBelle, Yolanda Adams, Aretha Franklin, and Whitney Houston. I wanted to dance with the enthusiasm and excitement of Debbie Allen, Beyoncé, and Michael Jackson. I wanted to preach to myself with the fire that comes from Bishop Noel Jones, Pastor Wayne Chaney, or Bishop T. D. Jakes. I wanted to continue to inspire people in the way of my mentors, Oprah and first lady Michelle Obama. I wanted to love with the unconditional love that only God had demonstrated to me. I wanted to truly *live*!

Recap:

- Divorce the drama.
- Get rid of everything that will prevent you from reorganizing your entire life.

- Don't resist the changes and adjustments.
- Live without regret!

Facing the Issues

I had never expected to have a breakdown. Perhaps it was arrogance or the belief that I was able to handle whatever came my way with no help. In order to understand what had just happened, I had to face the traumas that had taken place within an eighteen-month period. First, I had moved back to California and had taken on a new market as a corporate liaison. I had realized quickly that this new market was the opposite of the one that I had been in on the East Coast. My job performance had decreased, and my confidence had been compromised. Second, my health was failing, and I had no idea how to deal with many of the associated problems. My immediate family had no idea what I needed or how to give it to me. Finally, I was dealing with the breakup of a relationship with someone I had known for most of my life. The betrayal, the hurt, the regret, the deep pain, and the loss of innocence were all too much.

All these traumas resulted in me considering suicide. I felt as if death were the only way of dealing with my problems. I was humbled to the point of being speechless. At that moment, I thought: *If this is what rock bottom feels and looks like, then I humbly accept that title.*

I lived at rock bottom for months until the breakthrough came. You see, in the breakdown phase you have to get naked. You have to lose your pride and embrace the truth, no matter how revealing it is or how much it hurts.

Recap:

- Be honest with yourself and those around you.
- Conquer the issues one by one.
- Create a plan of action.
- Know that there is life after the pain.

walk in happiness and good health. Now that I am at this point, I am ready to face every issue, one by one. The pain and fear do not control me anymore!

Fear

In the breakthrough phase you have to conquer fear, anxiety, and pain. Fear is the emotion that you feel when you sense that you are in danger. It is a protective emotion that signals danger and helps you prepare for and cope with it. Fear includes physical, mental, and behavioral reactions. Fear is terror and panic. It is associated with dread and trepidation. Unproductive forms of fear will put you in bondage and cause you to make poor decisions. Fear will take your healthy choices away from you because you will make choices based only on the terror and the unknown. If you don't rise above the situation or individual that is controlling you through fear, you will be imprisoned by all the "what-ifs."

Some fears are healthy. For example, you may fear that if you continue to smoke you will get cancer. If you decide to stop smoking, then you have made a conscious decision to do something about a problem that could cause illness or even death. It's about taking control of the situation, and once you do that, your fear can no longer exist.

Then there are fears that arise from attachment or detachment, fears that arise from anger and hatred, and fears that you learn from your environment. Fear and anxiety exist when you find yourself being separated from something or someone you feel you need for your security or happiness. You can count on fear lurking nearby when you feel threatened by someone, which often leads to anger and hate. Oftentimes parents or other people in your immediate environment force their fears and anxieties upon you, and if you are vulnerable, you allow those fears to become a part of your development.

Overcoming your fears can be difficult. You must avoid believing that the fear you are experiencing is the absolute truth. You have to be prepared to take the risk that is preventing you from progressing. Make a list of all the things you would like to do, and if an item on your list will not kill you or harm you, you must truly examine why you have not accomplished it. Another way to overcome your fear is to think of all the different scenarios that could follow a decision that you are afraid of making. Once you address all the scenarios and responses, the fear will subside or disappear. Usually, once you commit to the process of examining your fears, you will begin to peel the layers until you get down to the root of the fear. And this is exactly when the fear begins to go away.

Anxiety is a very common feeling that accompanies fear. Anxiety occurs when you *worry* about the fear rather than *experience* the actual fear that accompanies an existing danger. Anxiety is a general term describing several disorders that cause nervousness, fear, apprehension, and worrying. Mild anxiety is vague and unsettling, while severe anxiety can be extremely debilitating and can have a major impact on daily life. When anxiety affects your sleeping patterns, your relationships, and your ability to work effectively, then professional intervention is needed.

Fear was one of the major issues that prevented me from being free. Being free and feeling free are essential to the success of a breakthrough. I had been suffering from fear since I was a little girl. I remember being terrified of speaking, of being honest, and of loving. I was afraid of rejection, of not pleasing my mother, of my own race, of failure, of being in public places—and all the things my mother taught me to be scared of. I was most terrified to be myself—to be comfortable in the freedom to express *my* thoughts, *my* wants, and *my* needs. When I decided to go through therapy, it opened up the door to freedom. Once that began to happen, I had to find the courage to embrace the truth about my past, my present, and my choices for my future.

I want you to know that when you decide to take control of your life and to address and conquer the fears that have crippled you, the people in your life will either walk away or be forced to adapt to the transformation that results from your taking a powerful stand. Focusing on positive areas that will increase your growth is the most important strategy when coping with friends and family members who have chosen to walk away. I suggest focusing on these areas:

- Yourself

- Your support team

- Forgiveness and moving forward

- Gratitude. Be thankful for every trial, because it will result in many lessons learned.

- Positive energy

When I began to break through all the drama, reality hit me head-on. I knew that reality consisted of all my fears, and I knew that I had to confront the people who had provoked them. Once I stood firm and submitted to my gut instincts and spiritual insight, I stood at the door of breakthrough, and I just had to walk through. As I stated before, the month of December was the beginning of the end. You see, before you reach the next phase in your journey, there is always a breaking point. My breaking point was Christmas Eve. At that time, I thought I was hitting the ultimate point in the breakdown phase, and I thought that as a result I would remain in pain, humiliation, anger, and stress. I broke through that Christmas Eve situation, and I experienced the joy of taking my power back.

When breakthrough comes, you think you are unprepared. You are not even aware that you are breaking through, until you realize that your response to adversity and pain is totally the opposite of how you have always responded. For me, thirty-eight years of responding in the same way came to an end. I realized that the definition of insanity is doing the same thing over and over and getting the same results. I realized that what I thought would hurt me—darn near kill me—didn't. The fear in that particular situation was gone, and I was hopeful that I could overcome my other fears.

When you are able to face the truth, the haters, the disappointments, and the fear, you are breaking through!

Recap:

Definition	Lessons
Emotion that you feel when you sense that you are in danger	Be prepared to take the risk that is preventing you from progressing.
Strong feeling of anxiety that exists when you find yourself being separated from something or someone you feel you need for your security or happiness.	Take control of your life; people will either walk away or adapt to your stand.

Pain

Pain is defined as an unpleasant sensory and emotional experience associated with actual or potential tissue damage. It is the feeling common to such experiences as stubbing a toe, burning a finger, putting iodine on a cut, and bumping the funny bone. But what about emotional pain? When you feel physical pain, you try to avoid situations that will do further damage, and you try to protect the area that has been hurt until it heals. Emotional pain can hurt worse than physical pain. Physical pain may heal rather quickly, but emotional pain can last for months, years, or even a lifetime if you don't address it and commit to the healing process.

"I want the pain to go away. Can anybody take this away? It hurts; I don't want it anymore. I wake up with it, I feel it throughout the day, and at times I go to sleep with it. Yes, physical and emotional pain is what I am facing. Is there a pill I can take, and every tear, pain in my body, and heartache will just go away and be replaced with peace and happiness?"

One day I was sitting in my therapist's office and expressing this. He looked me in the eye and said, "It's not supposed to just go away. It's supposed to be experienced, and once you get *through* the experience, you will have that peace and happiness you are looking for. It doesn't come with a quick fix."

My journey opened up my heart and my eyes to the real problem. I realized that I had been through so much pain and disappointment that I had become addicted to pain. I had no clue how to experience joy, because I had never known what joy felt like. I realized that my negative thoughts, once entertained, would only turn into negative confessions. I had been putting out into the universe many of these statements:

- I am in pain.

- I always attract people who hurt me and take advantage of me.

- I'm not the parent type (meaning that I'm not the prototype my mother suggests as a good mother).

- I'm sick, and I don't want to live in this pain.

- I always give, and I never receive anything in return.

- I will never get married again, nor do I want to.

- I am angry.

- I'll never be able to have total peace and happiness because of my past.

If you continue to put statements like these into the universe, then that is exactly what will happen. It seems so simple to say that *you are what you think and speak*. I know it's tempting to buy in to the fact that you are just stating reality, but the negative doesn't have to be the reality. Some people were begging me to speak positively, but I couldn't grasp what they were saying because I thought I was just telling the truth, *my* truth, and I didn't realize I had the ability to turn the whole situation around. All I needed to do was change my thoughts and words. It seems simple—but *boy*, did I have my work cut out for me! It's difficult to transform your mind.

The steps that I took to resolve my pain helped me to come full circle to the answers that I had known from the beginning. I had always had the solutions to several of my issues, but I didn't believe the solutions. In addition, I had no idea how to get to the solutions. It's a process, and it requires the appropriate steps. The length of the process and the quantity of steps needed depend on how long you resist what is true and positive for your life. If you continue to fight transformation, you will sink further and further into that black hole. Here are the nine steps I took to get past the pain and through the breakthrough phase:

1. Engage in healthy distractions that detour negative thoughts.

2. Focus on making each day a good day, no matter what happens.

3. Treat yourself as if *you* are what's most important; during this time it's all about you.

4. Tell yourself daily that the past cannot be redone and the future is an illusion, but the present is what you can use to make the biggest difference.

5. Do the right things for your health because good health, physical strength, and mental stability are needed to break through.

6. Practice yoga three times a week. If you get the endorphins working, your body produces dopamine, and that results in energy, peace, and happiness.

7. Go to the spa—and then go again!

8. Listen to music.

9. *Love* yourself, romance yourself, and respect yourself—and when you have mastered the art of this, give it to others.

The healing effect of music is amazing. I found that at different times music filled me with sadness, laughter, anger, anxiety, joy, and gratitude. At first I would fight against the emotions I felt when I heard certain music. But eventually, in the breakthrough phase, you're not in fight mode anymore. When the feelings make you scared, trigger pain from the past, or remind you of a person you loved, you are ready to explore those feelings and deal with them. You are ready to heal! Sometimes *every* song will remind you of a person you've lost, but you need to embrace the joy from that relationship and stop giving power to the pain. You have run from forgiveness for so long. Stop running *from* your destiny, and run *to* it instead.

When I was healing from emotional and physical pain, I listened to seven songs every week. These songs became my theme music for each day. These songs were my testimony. They gave me peace in the midst of the pain and after the broken pieces were mended. I share them with you and hope that they will help you too.

- Monday: "Let Go," sung by DeWayne Woods
- Tuesday: "I Love Me Better Than That," sung by Shirley Murdock
- Wednesday: "Just a Prayer Away," sung by Yolanda Adams
- Thursday: "Running Back to You," sung by Commissioned
- Friday: "One Night with the King," sung by Juanita Bynum
- Saturday: "Never Knew Love Like This Before," sung by Stephanie Mills
- Sunday: "Still I Rise," sung by Yolanda Adams

These songs touched my heart and forced me to be honest and totally open. They moved me to laugh again, smile again, be hopeful, love *me*, and have courage when fear showed up. People have asked me how I came up with the order of the songs, and there is no simple answer. With that said, each song was significant and related to each day.

Monday's song, "Let Go," set the tone of the week. Mondays were always the most hectic and filled with fires to put out. This song calmed me and made me feel that no matter what happened, God had the last say and had ordered my footsteps. Actually, this song was a big part of the transformation that took place in my mind.

I chose "I Love Me Better Than That" for Tuesday because I had to be extra sweet to myself and encourage myself after the drama that came with Mondays.

Wednesday was the middle of the week, and I needed to know then that my God—my higher power—was just a prayer away.

Thursday was usually the time of the week when I needed to be reassured. The anxiety that usually sent me running in the wrong direction would change its course when I heard this song, and I would find myself running back to my place of peace.

Thank God it's Friday! Friday was special for me. It was my time to pamper myself, to romance myself, and to love myself so that when the right man came along I would know how to receive him and give to him. The song "One Night with the King" was totally fitting. It made me feel romanced and protected. I would hear violins in the background—my favorite instrument—and I would just melt. The song emphasizes the fact that in one moment your life can change. Once you understand that living in the moment is *living*, you will understand that not living in the moment is *dying*!

On Saturday I needed something fun and upbeat, so I chose "Never Knew Love Like This Before." This song was very special to me, because when I first started writing a book several years ago, I called it *Never Knew Love Like This Before*.

Finally, on Sunday, "Still I Rise" was so appropriate. It was truly my testimony about my life, my journeys, my week, my trials, and all of my pain. It soothed me and assisted in the healing process.

You don't have to do it my way, with seven songs for the week; it may be that only one song will get you through. I needed those seven songs during my breakthrough phase, and they will forever be embedded in my heart. I was broken—so broken—and the words from each and every song spoke life to my life and ministered life's fresh fragrance. I couldn't get enough of positive thinking, because that's all I had to go on. I had been scared, in fear, at the bottom of life, and the negative had only pushed me further. The only thing left was positivity, and it was *free*, so I tried it! I never looked back. I proclaimed, "I want my joy back; I want my peace back; I want my strength back; I want my mind back; I want my self-esteem back; I want my hope back; I want my dreams back; I want my life back! I LOVE ME better than that—better than any relationship, any job, any physical illness, any lies, and anybody who doesn't want to be there. You are better than that. I am better than that."

Once I embraced this, I was at another breaking point. Yes—finally—I am ready to break out!

don't want to breeze through this as if it's an easy step because it's one of the hardest lessons that I have had to learn and endure through the many journeys that I have taken.

Forgiveness frees you from the pain associated with an act that has been imprisoning you for decades, years, months, days, or even moments. It gives you your smile back or makes it shine for the first time. It brings the ultimate feeling of liberation. It is the absolute definition of breakout. Once you have experienced forgiveness, you cannot ignore the transformation that your mind has gone through, and that transformation will lead you down the road of habitual forgiveness. You will forgive everyone and every action that has taken place in your life. Forgiveness is a gift for both you and the offending person.

You will not be able to break out fully or live according to your total purpose until you have embraced forgiveness. You must completely divorce the anger, the pain, the hurt, and the other negative emotions that are associated with your old circumstances. By no means am I stating that you will forget the painful thing that has happened, but you *can* free yourself of waking up and going to sleep with it every day. When the breakout experience happens, you not only learn from it but also use what you have learned to help change the lives of others. Your journey and life experiences are what lead to the breakout phase.

The Lesson

The lesson is that you cannot have freedom until you are living your purpose, and you are not living when you are in bondage. When you learn this lesson, you completely disassociate yourself from drama, negativity, lies, pain, and anything that kills your spirit and dreams. Every day the message of your purpose becomes clearer, and you realize that living in the moment is being fully present within it.

When you learn the lesson, you realize that you don't have to be perfect anymore. You don't even have to *try* to be perfect. You don't have to hide anymore. You can be who you are, and there is absolutely no reason ever to be something you're not, because you simply can't live a lie if you are walking in truth.

> The beginning of love is to let those we love be perfectly themselves, and not to twist them to fit our own image. Otherwise we love only the reflection of ourselves we find in them.
>
> —Thomas Merton

Breakout is the result of the work you did in breakthrough. You will know you are in this phase if you really learned the hard lessons of breaking through.

Overcoming

When I had my breakdown, I was experiencing intense panic attacks. I remember driving on the freeway, passing an exit that I had been taking for almost a year, and suffering a panic attack. I had to pull over, and I cried and did deep breathing. Once my mind was transforming to breakout, I learned to breathe through the panic as I approached the exit, and with tears falling from my eyes, I would find the courage to overcome it. In that particular situation, breakout happened one day when I took the exit without any thought and then stopped at a familiar Starbucks. As I was waiting in line, it hit me where I was, and I found that the feelings associated with the Starbucks were not painful anymore. I was surprised and proud of myself. As I got my feta-and-spinach wrap and chai iced tea, I smiled a huge smile and laughed out loud because I had broken out of that bondage!

On several occasions I faced challenges that tested the lessons I had learned in my breakthrough. One of those lessons was overcoming public opinion. I knew I had mastered this lesson when I was able to walk into an event at which I was the public speaker, look into the audience, spot people who had caused me harm, and still speak with love and confidence. When I truly connected with my purpose as speaker, which was fueled by passion, it resulted in nothing but love for myself and others. In that moment, all the pain these people had caused me no longer controlled me. I had not only broken through but also broken *out*—into my purpose.

I used to allow disappointments to sabotage an entire day, week, month, or season. But once I learned the lesson that living in the moment is the most important gift you can give yourself and the world, I began to break out. I was able to deal with disappointment *in the moment* and quickly move on to the next moment. The moment after I let disappointment go, it was replaced by gratitude. Why gratitude? Because I was thankful for the lesson I had learned: I was now able to move on. I was now finally living in the moment, and after thirty-nine years I had overcome the paralyzing effects of disappointment.

Alice Emerges from Wonderland

In a chapter of *Alice in Wonderland*, Alice is called up as a witness. She accidentally knocks over the jury box with the animals inside it, and the King of Hearts orders that the animals be placed back into their seats before the trial continues. Citing Rule 42 ("All persons more than a mile high to leave the court"), the King and Queen of Hearts order Alice to leave, but Alice refuses. She argues with the king and queen over the ridiculous proceedings. The queen shouts her familiar "Off with her head!" but Alice, unafraid, calls them out as just a pack of cards as they start to swarm over her. Alice's sister wakes her up for tea and brushes what turn out to be some leaves (not a shower of playing cards) off Alice's face. Alice leaves her sister on the bank to imagine all the curious happenings for herself.

This chapter reminded me of when I began to grow and transform, and people either wanted to stunt that growth or wanted me to leave the truth alone and continue to live a lie. Just like Alice, I got to a point where keeping quiet or condoning what was wrong was no longer an option. Alice doesn't care about titles; she proves that when she argues with the King and Queen of Hearts about what she feels is right, regardless of the queen's violent response. You see, when you stand up for yourself, and people know that they can't control you anymore, they sometimes respond by trying to destroy your credibility or kill your dream. I call these people *dream killers*.

Even when the cards are attempting to intimidate her, Alice stands up for herself. She has broken out of any fear that might have plagued her. She then wakes up out of Wonderland, which was all a dream, a fantasy.

I used to stress about so many situations because I pictured the worst possible outcome. Time and time again, it was not as bad as I had feared, and on many occasions it was quite the opposite of what I had assumed. When you allow fear to grip your heart and overtake your decision making, the result will always be negative and illusory. Once I stood up to what I feared the most, I was back in control. The fear was in its proper place. It was an illusion, and I had broken out of its bondage.

I remember being seven years old and watching *All My Children* with my mother. I was becoming addicted to a soap opera at a young age, and both the addiction and the fantasy world of the show were grooming my personality. I truly believed that I was the black Erica Kane. Erica was a brilliant, adventurous, powerful businesswoman and a go-getter. She was always the center of attention, dressed for greatness, and the picture of sophistication. She was beautiful, even when she went to bed and woke up. I began to emulate Erica and to identify with her outlook on relationships. She was a great actress and seemed to mesmerize men, but her relationships were always short-lived and full of drama. One of her love interests, Jack, stood out to me. He loved Erica and was strong enough to deal with her large personality. A successful lawyer, he was unbelievably charming—not to mention easy on the eyes. I fell in love with Erica so completely that I felt she was a family member. That's how real her character was to me.

Can you say, "Alice, come out of Wonderland?" You guessed it: I was Alice, and I was stuck in *All My Children* Wonderland. I would dress up just to sit in my own house. I studied Susan Lucci's sophistication, as well as that of other women such as Lena Horne and Diahann Carroll. As I grew into a woman, I bought beautiful lingerie and made sure that I looked lovely even as my head hit the pillow. I was a childhood actress until the age of eighteen, and I must say I was great at the craft.

The downside was that I was so caught up in the fantasy world of Erica Kane that I believed real life was the same. On the soap operas anything could happen, but that generally did not reflect real-life situations. It definitely didn't prepare me for the "real" world—but then again, that wasn't the show's responsibility. As I looked for my fantasy Jack in every relationship, I was disappointed over and over again. I often found myself asking, "Where is my Jack? Why aren't *you* acting like Jack? Why don't you fly me on your jet to a romantic location for dinner? Why aren't you patient like Jack? Why can't you work all day and have a candlelight dinner waiting for me when I get home? Why can't you emotionally fill me up?" I know I sounded like a two-year-old jumping up and down and having a tantrum. I discovered the truth that Jack was a character and so was Erica. My life was real, and judging by the way life was going, it was going to stay that way.

I was in Wonderland for a long time. I now realize that some of the expectations I placed on my relationships—whether romance or friendship—were unrealistic. There is nothing wrong with having expectations, but it's important to keep them realistic. If a man is a great guy, and perhaps he is romantic three times a month instead of every day, he isn't necessarily a failure. If your man has a strong work ethic and doesn't cater to your every need every day after a stressful or long day of work, he isn't necessarily inconsiderate. If he is considerate of your feelings in general, you have found someone special.

For years I placed a tremendous amount of pressure on my partners to perform like all the leading men I'd watched—the knights in shining armor. But along the way, reality kept hitting: my dad died suddenly; I was diagnosed with carcinoma in situ of the cervix; and I faced paralysis, extreme financial loss, a plethora of breakups, dyslexia, molestation, and thoughts of suicide. I realized that these issues were parts of my life—*real* life.

As I began to break through all of my trials, I started to realize that a healthy relationship occurs when two people share respect, trust, honesty, support, equality, separate identities, good communication, spiritual connection, and a sense of playfulness. I now know that my knight in shining armor is the ability to love in sickness and in health, for better or for worse, and to love and cherish, for richer and for poorer, till death do us part. Sorry, Jack, I am no longer in Wonderland, and my name is not Alice. It's Michelle "Breakout" Hannah.

Sleeping Beauty *or* Sleeping with the Enemy

"Sleeping Beauty" is a fairy tale that is familiar to most of us, but I doubt that you have closely evaluated the story and thought about how our lives play it out. I will briefly outline the story in order to provide a working synopsis:

- A baby princess is born, and an angry fairy attempts to put a curse on the child.

- The curse states that when the girl is sixteen, she will prick her finger on a spindle and die.

- A good fairy intercedes and says that when the princess hurts herself, she will not die but fall into a deep sleep.

- Her mother, the queen, tries to keep the princess away from spindles.

- The princess observes a servant spinning and tries it, but she pricks herself and falls into a deep sleep.

- The queen is told that love is the only thing that can wake the princess.

- When the queen finds out that it could take up to a hundred years for the princess to wake up, she becomes heartbroken and dies.

- A fairy casts a spell on the rest of the people who dwell in the castle so that they will all be asleep with the princess.

- Years pass; grass, shrubs, and trees grow; and the castle becomes hidden behind them.

- A handsome prince lives close by. He is depressed and is looking for peace. He sees a forest, explores it, and makes his way through it.

- The prince sees the castle. He thinks everyone is dead but comes to understand that they are just asleep.

- The prince sees the princess. In her face he sees the serenity, peace, and purity he is looking for.

- The prince kisses the princess, and she awakes because her love has come. They marry and live happily ever after.

Many times we are fed the "happily ever after" line, but nothing is that black and white in life. Sometimes circumstances shake our very foundations and either build our characters or break us down. If we are not prepared, oftentimes we do not recover. It is possible to be happy, but to imply that everything will be perfect if we find love (or love finds us) is totally misleading.

When I first heard this story it was just a fairy tale to me, but when I read it recently it meant something totally different. It was full of lessons and wisdom. I noticed so many new twists. First, there is no king—no father in the house—which means that the queen is a single mother making decisions and paying for the staff in the castle on her own. I'm sure she is so busy that she doesn't have time to run a background check on everybody, so of course some haters slip through the cracks. She has no clue that an employee might put a curse on her daughter and cause the princess to fall into a deadly sleep for such a long time. When you are a single parent, the responsibility is so great that you often miss the details. I wonder if the outcome of "Sleeping Beauty" would have been different if a father were in the home. I truly believe that two sound heads are better than one. I think back to my own experience, and I truly believe that if I had always had a great husband, or perhaps an active father, many decisions and events would not have had the negative results they did.

Another "aha" moment for me was noticing that the prince lives so close by. Isn't it funny when something is right under your nose? His fight to find out what is behind the weeds and grass symbolizes his courage. His discouragement comes when he is working hard to get through all the trees, grass, and weeds but doesn't seem to be succeeding. Then the breakthrough comes, and he sees a castle beyond all the tangled trees and darkness. Once he sees the princess, he finds everything he has longed for. When a man knows he has found what he is looking for, more than likely it moves him to make a decision. The prince's decision is to marry Sleeping Beauty, and it is his love for her that wakes her from her deep sleep.

Many times in my life I was so hurt that I was asleep to all that was going on around me—including warning signs. I simply checked out. When you begin to break through, you wake up and transform. When you break out, you divorce the idea of "happily ever after," but you embrace the innate joy that doesn't change simply because your circumstances make you happy or sad at any given moment. You break away from someone else's false definition of a successful relationship. When you break out, you decide not to sleep with the enemy.

Unbreakable

Unbreakable is defined as "impossible to destroy, especially under ordinary usage; able to withstand rough usage; able to withstand an attempt to

destroy." I would like to focus on the second and third definitions.

What does it mean to "withstand rough usage"? It means to endure and survive a violent and forceful action. On life's journey there will be many actions that question your foundations. When you decide to embrace transformation, however, the heat gets turned up. The actions that take place are not just regular storms; they are violent and forceful ones. Whether you want to deal with the brutal effects or not, you are forced to face them. We all go through some violent storms because of our own choices, but there are also storms that are beyond our control.

Once you understand what it is to withstand rough usage, you must also understand what it means to withstand an attempt to destroy you. Once you endure and survive forceful action, you have endured any challenge to shatter your being. You have survived the adverse situations that were needed to rip apart the negative aspects of your life and personality so that positivity could illuminate your state of being.

I received a card one day, at a moment when I was feeling that no one appreciated me. The first line read, "Little Red Riding Hood, the first woman to ride with wolves." I immediately felt empowered and moved to read the story. It amazed me that Little Red Riding Hood was given two instructions from her mother—don't dawdle and don't talk to strangers—but then she disobeyed them both. The story states that Riding Hood was so distracted that she didn't see the wolf, and he did everything he could to sound friendly when he spoke to her. Little Red Riding Hood gave the wolf all the information he needed because he made her feel comfortable. Once he had the information, he ran with it to Grandmother's house. Thinking that the soft knock at the door was her granddaughter, Grandmother told the wolf to come in, and of course, he entered and gobbled her up.

Do you give too much information to people who don't have your best interests in mind? Being a woman, do you fall for that sweet and smooth line from a man, only to find out he is nothing but a wolf? Do you receive the best advice from people who love you but then disobey them and get distracted? And on the road of distraction, do you meet a pack of wolves or a situation that results in an attempt to devour your life?

At the end of the story, the wolf dressed up in Grandmother's clothes right after he ate her. *Where is this wolf's conscience?* you may ask. He then waited for Little Red Riding Hood to arrive. She showed up and realized that this was not her grandmother because if there is one thing about love, it's that it's familiar. In addition, a wolf can only pretend for so long, and then he has to show his teeth. Once Little Red Riding Hood discovered who the wolf was, she ran crying for help. She learned several great lessons: she should listen to instructions from loved ones, and there are negative consequences to bad decisions. The most important lesson I learned from this story was that no matter how loudly the wolf roared in my life, or how often that wolf might have attempted to kill me, I discovered, thankfully, that I am unbreakable.

Breakout happens when you have finally embraced life's many changes and have become willing to live your purpose by any means necessary. You are willing to do the work that it takes to live in the moment while living your purpose every day.

This is where sacrifice and selfishness meet on the same road. The sacrifice is the dedication and work that are required to achieve balance and to live your purpose. But during this time you might be viewed as selfish, and you are. Others start to sense a certain synergy when you are in the breakout phase; breakout is infectious, and people want to be around you. They want to be the priority in your life. However, you have to make some hard decisions, which are usually the unpopular ones that disappoint people. You have to be selfish and decline attractive invitations consistently. Your goals, your plan, and the energy and peace it takes to achieve them will at times isolate you, and if that defines selfishness, then selfishness is not negative.

Once you achieve balance, peace, and living in the moment, and once you have identified the right energies to maintain your purpose, you are fully involved in breakout.

Chapter 5

Break It!

We all have bad habits and realize that they need to broken. But here is the ultimate question: Are you ready to commit to the work of breaking the habit? In this chapter I will discuss five bad habits that I struggled with and the steps I took to conquer the control these bad habits had over me. Breaking these habits resulted in my breaking free.

Habits are behaviors or tendencies formed through repetition. People who have harmful habits are often aware of the consequences and risks to their well-being. It takes about twenty-one days of determination and discipline to change an old habit or to form a new one. Habits that have been ingrained more deeply in the brain take a lot longer to break.

If you want to change a bad habit, you will need to identify the triggers that motivate the habit, the intention of the behavior, and the benefit of getting rid of it. The bottom line is that you must commit to breaking it! You must break whatever is preventing you from living and walking in total freedom.

Breaking bad habits is a process. The acknowledgment usually happens in the breakdown phase. The commitment to change comes in the breakthrough phase. Finally, your breakout is the evidence that the habit has been broken.

I had several bad habits that I was ready to break and needed to break. I knew I had to overcome them in order to maintain a healthy mental and physical state. We all have bad habits, and we know that a select few of them prevent us from transforming. You might not have any of the habits that I discuss below, but take time to reflect and to address the ones you *do* have. Change is not easy, but it is necessary!

Negativity about Your Own Life

Being negative about my life was the norm, but I was positive about everyone else's life. It was a very bad habit that I had struggled with for years. I could never see the positivity in my own life, because there had been so much disappointment and pain. I guess you can say that I was a cheerleader and true optimist regarding anyone but myself. Although I had confronted many obstacles and had overcome so many tragedies, I still felt an unbelievable lack of accomplishment. It was easier to experience positive feelings through other people's circumstances.

In 2009, someone I was very close to expressed that I was a negative person, and I was beyond appalled. After all, I had been very positive and helpful toward people who were in physical, emotional, and financial pain. I had sacrificed so much in order to display nothing but positivity. But, after thinking about it, I had to admit that the person was right: I was negative about my own life. I was used to constant drama, and I had become addicted to pain. No one understood that I truly wanted to be addicted to joy and happiness. It was very challenging to break this bad habit, especially since the habit had existed for more than twenty years.

Solutions

I started by doing something positive for myself every day. Here are some examples of what I did:

- Declared positive affirmations about my life. One daily positive affirmation turned into two, and eventually two grew to several positive statements that I could honestly say and feel about my life and myself.

- Stopped the negative thought process before speaking it into the universe.

- Spoke the positive thought before the negative thought made it to my lips.

- Filled my environment with all the beautiful things that made me smile, such as gardenias and tulips. I didn't wait for anyone to buy them for me; I bought them for myself as needed.

- Made the most of what I had in front of me. Because I had moved to California, I could no longer enjoy the beautiful flags at the monument that had given me so much peace and serenity in Washington DC. But there was a flag on my balcony, and I had a video of a flag blowing in the wind, so I utilized what I had.

- Focused daily on gratitude. (To behold God's wonderful land—sunsets, sunrises, and unbelievable views—is truly the way to my heart, and I am thankful that I can do it.) I took the initiative and found some of the most wonderful views in California to enjoy every week. Surrounding myself with positive affirmations and scenery ushered in peace and gratitude for God's miracles and awesome land.

The hardest part of the solution was surrounding myself with positive people and divorcing all the negative people in my life. Did you know that a person can be a positive individual but be a negative influence in your life? It's about what fits for you. If a person is unhealthy for you, then you have to make some tough decisions. Remember, it's all about you and your well-being.

I don't know if I broke my habit in twenty-one days, but I will say this: every day that I committed to working on it was a day for the better. Within a couple of months, I observed that I had begun to see myself in a more positive way than ever before.

If you do the work, I promise it will result in nothing but greatness!

Interrupting

Being a good listener does not just mean staying quiet until you get your turn to speak. It means truly listening to what an individual has to say.

It means caring about what that individual is feeling and how he or she is looking to grow from the situation at hand. When you respect people, you do not interrupt them.

As I got older, I realized that I was not a good listener. I had a problem with interrupting, and I tended to monopolize conversations. I was amused when I noticed that the people closest to me had this habit too, and it drove me nuts. Isn't it funny how we end up copying the behaviors we dislike in our parents and close friends?

I realized that my need for control was what drove me to monopolize conversations. Believe it or not, you cannot control people—especially grown-ups—and frankly, why would you want to? A mature relationship isn't about control; it's about mutual respect. Trust me: being a good listener is a true skill, and it takes practice. Interrupting is an extremely bad habit, which has to be broken if your relationship is to be healthy.

This habit took some time to break. I must admit, it was most difficult to be a fully present and unselfish listener. No matter how much you want to defend yourself or jump in, you have to think about how disruptive that is and how disrespectful to the individual who is attempting to express how he feels and what is important to him. When you interrupt, it's as if you are saying that nothing the speaker expresses is important. Acknowledgment goes a long way, and when an individual doesn't feel acknowledged, it is truly painful, and there is no closure. The speaker ends up carrying that pain around for days, months, and sometimes years. Listening, acknowledging, not interrupting, and not monopolizing the conversation are all essential factors of healthy communication.

Solutions

After attending several therapy sessions and reading many books, I came up with techniques that worked for me. I shared these techniques with friends and associates who had the same issues, and to my surprise, they have all had great results. These are the techniques that I used to break the bad habit of interrupting:

- **B**e dedicated to being an unselfish listener.

- **R**espond with love.

- **E**mpathy and compassion are traits that you must communicate verbally and nonverbally.

- **A**sk if it's okay to take notes so that you won't forget to address all of your concerns.

- **K**eep an open mind.

Listening to Gossip

I am not one to spread gossip, but I used to do something just as bad: I *listened* to gossip. Even if it was for just a short period of time, I listened. Listening to gossip is just as damaging as doing the gossiping because you are lending an ear to the trash dump. Gossip is so hurtful because the story is inaccurate 90 percent of the time. I have learned that how a person perceives a situation does not necessarily match reality. I once heard that there are three sides to any story: yours, theirs, and the truth. When you are the recipient of secondhand information, you should never pass judgment or spread the story to someone else.

Gossip involves repeating talk about others' private affairs. Sometimes people start rumors that are intended to harm or to criticize a person. People who gossip use this destructive chatter to make themselves feel better about their positions in life. Healthy discussion is focused on more constructive conversation; you may be discussing something going on in another person's life, but you are not doing it at his or her expense. Bearers of gossip cannot be trusted; your secrets will never be safe with them. Just as they have betrayed other people's trust they will betray yours.

Once I became aware that listening to gossip was a bad habit, I had to reflect on the reasons for my behavior. What I found was very difficult to face: It made me feel better about my own life to hear about the misfortune of someone else. I was so depressed about my own life and embarrassed about my mistakes that it made me feel better to hear that someone was worse off than I was. What a hypocrite I was: I wouldn't gossip about others, but I would listen to the gossip of others and sometimes comment on it. As with most gossip, I never heard all sides of the story.

The excuse of wanting to be well informed and wanting to know everything that happens around you is just that: an excuse to gossip. Presently, when I hear someone say "he said" or "she said," it turns my stomach. Why is it that the source of the gossip is never named? Gossipers claim they don't want to tell you the name because they don't want to get a big mess started; well, the mess started when the gossip was first introduced.

Sometimes people tear you apart in order to make themselves look innocent or to paint themselves as victims. They don't seem to consider the fact that words can destroy your spirit. I was in a place in life where I was broken and broken down, and the gossip that certain people initiated pushed me dead-on into that breaking point. While this wasn't nearly all that led to the breakdown, it was definitely a part of it.

Solutions

To address this habit, I not only had to take responsibility for my behavior but also had to ensure that the gossiper was clear that I would not participate in any garbage dumping. I had to keep these factors in mind at all times. I hope that the following suggestions help you to overcome this bad habit:

- If the conversation is not positive, shut it down!
- Put yourself in the position of the person who is being targeted by the gossiper.
- Be aware that the gossiper is spreading negative, not innocent, information. Remember that if you listen, you are contributing to the hurt that may result.

- If the conversation could cause harmful perceptions about the individual, it could lead you to false conclusions.

- If you listen and give feedback, you must expect that the gossiper will repeat everything you say. Your contribution will be repeated not word for word but according to the gossiper's preferred interpretation.

- Do not passively listen to gossip. It implies agreement.

Sugar

I was once addicted to sugar. If I didn't have it, my moods and judgment would be affected. I would be irritable and would get headaches. On the other hand, sugar seemed to be the answer to comforting me and giving me temporary happiness. When you are addicted to something, it doesn't matter how it affects you, because you're hooked. I was aware that cancer feeds on sugar, but did that stop me? No—I kept on consuming it. Hershey's Milk Chocolate with Almonds, Peanut M&M's, and cupcakes were my favorites. Just writing about these foods brings a familiar smile to my face.

I had to wean myself from sugar, but because sugar is in almost everything, it was almost impossible to get it out of my diet completely. However, I did feel totally different once I kicked the habit of having it every day. My thinking was much clearer, and I was less constipated. Let me tell you, when you are constipated, it truly affects how you feel and how you react. When my bowels are free-flowing and I have a healthy colon, I have the same euphoric feeling I used to have when I ate a cupcake. But it takes self-discipline to say no and to reach instead for something that is truly nourishing for your body.

Solutions

- Grab a piece of fruit instead of a cookie.

- Treat yourself to a sugary treat *one* day out of the week instead of every day.

- Try ChromeMate for help with sugar cravings.
- Address the emotional issues instead of feeding them with sugar.

Negative Generational Influences

Some bad habits come from generational influences. In no way am I saying that just because your mother or father was an alcoholic or a drug addict you will become one too—but the chances are definitely higher. Whether we like it or not, as children we learn behaviors from our parents. The patterns that our parents and grandparents demonstrate might reach back several generations. Our parents, grandparents, and great-grandparents didn't have the tools that we now have to deal with our problems and to navigate through life. The truth is, most of our family members probably would have benefitted from some form of therapy.

We have to be aware of those patterns that are not going to enhance our lives, and we must not accept those patterns as our own or pass them to the next generation. We have to remember not to blame our parents or their parents; their behavior reflects years of conditioning. Acceptance is crucial to growth, and we must accept both who we are and who our families are. It's highly unlikely that we can change who our parents are, but we *can* change who we are and decide who we don't want to be.

Forgiveness is the key to peace and happiness. Forgiving is one of the hardest things to do, but we must confront everything that has happened to us to bring us to this breaking point in life. We must let go of the things that have hurt us and no longer serve us. Forgiveness of past generations is no quick fix, and it takes time, but I promise you that if you embrace the process, you will be free!

Solutions

If you want to shed negative generational influences, try these strategies:

- Develop a positive self-image, and disengage from how others view you.

- Know that you are responsible for your own decisions, independent of how you were raised. You have the power to take control of your life and not to allow your past environment to control your destiny.

- Choose to speak, see, hear, and feel only what feels great to you. Healthy interaction feels good and balanced. If it doesn't feel good, it's not!

Breaking It Results in Breaking Free!

Breaking it—whatever "it" is—will result in breaking free. Once you acknowledge problems, accept what you cannot change, break bad habits, forgive those who have hurt you, and destroy every negative thought with a couple of positive thoughts, you will begin to feel free. When you make the choice to *break it,* you make the choice never to repeat it. You will be in a place of honesty as never before. You will no longer have to hide behind fear or lies.

Freedom is the ability to be comfortable in your own skin. You are free when you are at peace with what makes you happy and someone else's beliefs—no matter how close they are or how much you love them—don't affect your overall peace. When you are free in your mind, you will be free to welcome your purpose and to live it. Get out of the way so that God can make a way.

Chapter 6

Love Breaks

A love break means taking a break to show love through hugging, kissing, making love, walking in the park, or any other act of love or intimacy. When do you take a love break? When the situation becomes too tense and love is not being shown. You will find ways to overcome the challenges that are presented when you attempt to take a love break. Real love will step in, because when you truly love someone, you can always find the strength to take a love break.

You will learn about working, parent-child, and couples love breaks. Most of all, you will be excited to start taking love breaks.

This chapter is very intimate and close to my heart. I hope you enjoy reading it as thoroughly as I have enjoyed writing it. I have always been fascinated by the definition of *love*, the attributes of it, the action, and ultimately the experience. On this lifelong journey I realized that in every relationship there has to be a moment that you take away and enjoy, whether it's taking a moment to love yourself, to show love to someone else, or to receive love. I have found that on the journey to find the greatest love, I had to look within. How could I expect anyone to love me deeply the way I needed, or to give me the attention that I needed, when I had no clue how to do that for myself? It comes back to self-worth. When you know that you are worthy of receiving love, giving it will come from the most sincere place. There is nothing greater than the love of God, but if we believe that God dwells within us, then self-love is essential to the journey of defining true love.

After getting divorced, I read the vows that people take to be married and became determined to respect the importance of those vows if I ever had an opportunity to take them again. You see, I believe that those vows start long before you are married. The marriage is a fulfillment of honoring God and a way to make a partnership legal in the eyes of humankind. I had failed at marriage and lost any hope of a healthy relationship. I had lost much in past relationships but had gained so much more. I would even say that these relationships motivated some life changes that eventually worked together for my good.

One particular relationship was full of many ups and downs that resulted in love breaks. I was finally in a place of submitting to a better way to deal with conflict. Oftentimes, when I would be confronted with a tense moment I would shut down. In this particular relationship he would respond the same. As a result, when two people shut down at the same time, communication has ceased. However when you have the desire to work at your relationship, you will try different tools that will overcome the challenges. The most effective tool was taking a love break. We committed that when the moment was tense or anger was present, one of us had to introduce a love break. Did it work every time? No, but it diffused many potential arguments. If you can make love breaks part of the foundation of your relationship, half the battle is won.

A love break is not only for an intense moment or for romantic relationships. You can use it for any relationship. I use love breaks with my daughter, who just recently became a teenager. You know how it is to live with someone going through puberty. When I reach a point where I am about to scream, we take a love break, which usually consists of sharing a hug or doing something fun. It takes the negativity or tension out of the situation. I use this technique with my friends, and I know that it is infectious because now they are taking love breaks with their families. I have who friends use them not only to diffuse a negative situation but also just to show some love. Some friends who are honeymooners take love breaks all the time.

Some people have asked me, "Do you need to announce that you are taking a love break, or do you just do it?" Well, you have to consider how men and women tend to feel about how a love break is introduced. When a woman says, "We need a love break," men usually feel defensive or start strategizing next steps to fix something. If a woman makes the announcement in frustration or anger, the tone is all wrong. Women crave a moment to nurture, to connect emotionally, and to break the silence. At especially tense times, perhaps love breaks should just be *done,* not announced. Your partner or friend will understand what you are doing: showing love in order to break the negativity and guide in the positivity. When you are in a long-distance relationship, or if you travel as part of your profession, physical love breaks are not always possible. In other words, you can't just walk over and kiss, hug, or massage your partner. In this case, you may have to announce the love break: "Baby, let's nip this in the bud and concentrate on nothing but love in this moment." I promise you, it will set the stage to deal with the issues that come with any relationship. No matter what the outcome, you will have the peace of knowing that your decisions came from love, not anger.

I would like to share some touching stories that others have related regarding my love break technique. My hope is that you will have some great examples to follow and learn from.

Working Love Breaks

A friend of mine thought love breaks were a little comical at first, but as he began to understand their meaning, he realized that they were very beneficial in his work environment. When one of his employees was out of line, he would suggest they take a walk, which was his version of a love break. If he allowed intense moments to worsen instead of initiating a love break, the consequences could include loss of employment for his workers. My friend initiates these walks out of love. He also cares enough to correct his employees when they are wrong and to give them solutions on how to proceed in a positive way.

My friend states that the most important thing to remember in taking this type of love break is that the offense is forgiven, and once you reenter the doors of your office, the issue is over. That's what love is about: forgiveness, correction, selflessness, and fairness.

Parent-Child Love Breaks

As parents, we sometimes get caught up in discipline, correction, and the need to protect our children from everything that could hurt them. We may forget what is most important, and that is showing love during the intense moments of our children's lives.

Most of us have either raised a teenager or been around a teenager at some point, and we realize that they go through many changes, sometimes within a twenty-four-hour period. They have extreme mood swings; they battle with acceptance while trying to maintain their individuality; and their hormones are all over the place. We try to relate and remember how we felt at that age, and at times the word *challenge* is an understatement. Can you say, "Love break?"

My friends and I have found that taking love breaks with our children has helped us shed the negative emotions that parents and their children experience. When you are feeling an intense moment with your child or teenager, that is the time to initiate a love break. It could be a fun activity, a hug, kisses (be prepared for your teenager to respond with embarrassment), or simple acknowledgment of your child's concerns and fears. My friends and I have experienced nothing but positive outcomes from parent-child love breaks. When you show and give love, I guarantee you that it will be returned somehow.

Couples Love Breaks

A couple I know had a lot of passion, and their disagreements were just as intense as was their love. When both parties knew they were about to say something they were going to regret, or when they experienced a major breakdown in communication, they would take a love break. They stated that these breaks provided some of their most intimate and pure moments. This was where they met on the road of forgiveness and restoration. This was how they made peace with all the complexities of the situation. This was their no-judgment zone. No matter how much they had been through, in that precious moment they experienced the intimacy and the action of

love. They were living in the moment, and they discovered that love is not how much you can take but how much you can give.

When you experience genuine love breaks, they become like air: they are essential in order for your relationship to breathe. Your love breaks may involve taking a weekend getaway, taking a break from the kids, or taking time off from your job. What's important is that you refocus on what is most important: loving each other from the inside out. When you are truly in love and fully present within it, love breaks are those moments when you are free of the muddy waters and restored with joy. No matter what the monumental effects of adversity may be, you are able to love that individual where he or she is in the moment, and you have strong faith in the future.

In December 2010, an idea hit me, and I immediately reserved the domain name *thelovebreak.com*. The idea was to create marketing materials with adorable sayings that related to taking a love break. Some of the sayings were as follows:

- Take a Break and Love Me
- Take a Break and Stop FUSSING
- Take a Break and SMILE
- STOP! Take a Love Break
- Pucker Up! It's Time for a Love Break
- Love Break! Unfold Your Arms, Wrap Them around Me

I was so excited about this idea because I had always been fascinated by showing love and teaching others how to do so. This was a movement that I was introducing to the world, and it was thrilling to think that my setbacks were truly going to be my comeback. This idea kept growing, from marketing the Love Break line to creating a blog called *In the Moment* to crafting the home page—where you can purchase my book and find out all you need to know about our seminars, conferences, and community involvement. So please, stop by thelovebreak.com. I promise that you will not leave without feeling loved.

Chapter 7

This Is Transformation

Transformation is a change in nature, function, or a current condition. There is nothing subtle about true transformation; it's drastic, radical, and thorough. To me, *thorough* means painstaking, detailed, and systematic. Transformation results from the breakups, the ultimate breakdown, and the multiple breakthroughs. It ushers you toward the courage it takes to break out.

In this chapter, I will define transformation and explore the results of this phase through personal stories. You will feel as though you have had a makeover after reading this chapter. The section called "Hoodie to Heels" explains how I went from wearing dark hoodies during my darkest moments to wearing bright colors and fabulous heels. You will take an adventurous transformation voyage with me from beginning to end. Through *evolving*, you will grow and be fully present within love. The steps of transformation will help you blossom and live in every moment.

What Transformation Looks Like

If you are destined for greatness, your transformation will be a journey that causes every emotion possible—even emotions that you didn't know were possible—to surface. At times you will feel you can't make it for one more moment, but once you are in position for true transformation, you realize that making it is the only option. You will have to embrace a radical shift in your life, and trust me: although your circumstances may or may not change the way you want them to, there will be a change, and that change is you. A big part of the change is that you will respond differently.

As I began to get comfortable in my transformation, my skin changed; it became smoother, clearer, and more youthful. My physical body changed inside and out. I wasn't obsessing about wanting to be a size 4 anymore. Instead, I welcomed my curves, and the flat stomach that I had been willing to pay for—along with the breast lift that at one time I couldn't wait to get—was becoming a distant memory. The transformation began in my mind, and soon I was comfortable in my journey. Eating healthful foods and exercising became exciting and no longer felt like chores.

My physical body, which had been the opposite of healthy, began to line up with what I spoke into existence: "I am healthy and happy." Yes, I willed it into my life—the total healing of my body and my mind. When you get your emotions in check, all that is crooked straightens up. I looked in the mirror for the first time, and I loved every bit of my size 6 body, 34DDD breasts, thirty-seven-inch hips, and twenty-seven-inch waist. They were *me*; I had finally transformed into a healthy, confident woman, and I was wearing out the term *sexy*.

This is what transformation looks like.

Remember that your journey will be different from everyone else's. It can last two months, two years, or twenty years; it depends on you. How you react to the steps of your journey, and how quickly you learn its lessons, is also up to you.

Hoodie to Heels

You're probably wondering, "What does she mean by hoodie to heels?" Well, I will not leave you in suspense any longer. When I was in my breakup and breakdown phases, I wore a hoodie—black, navy blue, and *beautiful* charcoal gray—accompanied by matching sweatpants. What a fashionista! I was going through a mourning and adjustment phase, and the hoodies were my way of hiding my uncombed hair and camouflaging my puffy eyes. The sweats were to hide the weight gain in the breakup phase and to hide the weight loss in the breakdown phase. Due to the time I'd fractured three bones in my foot, I couldn't wear heels, so it was right up my alley to be completely comfortable in my Nike tennis shoes.

Before my injury I had been very attached to my heels, and when I had to stop wearing them I fell deeper into a depression. I had lived my life by the motto "You don't have to look how you feel," so I always made sure I looked great no matter how I felt. In my breakup phase, for the first time in my life I didn't care about looking good, because I couldn't wear the one thing that made me feel like a sexy woman: my heels. I realized at that moment that my heels defined a certain part of who I thought I was. I had no clue how to rock an outfit without heels. How could I look fly with flats? So, with depression knocking at the door, I opened it wide and embraced it with my hoodie and sweats.

Thank God for breakthrough, because once the metamorphosis started with the renewing of my mind, I realized that I wanted to become closely acquainted with real colors again. No matter how bright or how soft it was, I needed color. I was ready to break through, from hoodie to heels. It began with bright and refreshing fashions. Then the challenge was to find some hot flats that felt and looked good. I learned that feeling like a sexy woman was a state of mind that was not based on my heels. And I learned that I *can* look confident and unique in a hot pair of flats—specifically, Christian Louboutin ballerina slippers. Now *that's* transformation!

Why Christian Louboutin? I have always considered myself innovative, and during my transformation I had to be willing to reinvent myself. Christian Louboutin understands fully what it is to be a groundbreaking pioneer of originality. My new life broke all the rules. I was dancing to my own music, which ultimately was created by God. I found that Mr. Louboutin's shoes made me feel confident and empowered, and that feeling aligned with how I chose to live the rest of my life.

Your hoodie-to-heels moment might be totally different from mine, but nevertheless, the point is that you must give up something to gain so much

more. Know that when you are ready to leave what has been familiar to you during your relationship with colorless days, you will welcome a life of vibrant colors. There will be different shades to represent the different journeys. I can guarantee you that the lessons you learn will make the transformation worthwhile.

Breakout was the action of my transformation. I was out of my hoodie, which had held hands with all the effects of pain, anxiety, anger, and fear. I was healed physically and mentally. My foot was finally ready to slide back into my heels—but not just any heels. I traded in my hoodie for freedom and the embrace of my purpose, and I celebrated the moment with a new pair of shoes. There is nothing like enjoying the peace of God, being physically fit, feeling happy from the inside out, loving, and living in the moment … and a great pair of heels.

What Transformation Feels Like

Transformation will position you to be finally ready for love that is unconditional. I never thought that I would find the closest reflection of God until I met the man (my special friend) who loved me through it all. I had the pleasure of meeting him during my transformation phase, and he could feel my transformation. True transformation is powerful, and the power of the laws of attraction—and of God—was as real as each breath I took. I'd always wondered how I would react when unconditional love made itself known. What would I be wearing? Would I be at my ideal weight? Would I have all the material things I wanted? You see, when you are truly transformed—which means you are walking in your purpose— you're happy with who you are, you're confident, and you're being led by your higher power. Nothing about your life is superficial. You are on the road of restoration, joy, complete sanity, inner peace, and love.

True love corrects us when we are wrong. My special friend, who I call my endearment, listens when I need to vent, even if the venting is about him. He knows just what it takes to calm me and to balance me. His wisdom is well beyond his years. I remember one night he expressed to me that I needed to say something about a certain situation, but it was important to find the right time to say it. Timing is everything. He suggested that no matter how upset I was, I should take some time and think about it before I spoke. "Take a love break and just love me," he was saying. "More than likely, by the time you confront the situation, the anger and frustration will be taken out of it." He was basically telling me to take my own advice: take a love break when I am feeling tense, or have a need to defend myself or to inform someone of his or her offense.

Transformation occurs the moment you no longer feel the need to defend or to fight back; change has arrested your resistance. I am so thankful that I met someone whom I truly respected, someone who gave me the best kind of love: correction, restoration, and a sweet gentleness that comes very close to the image of God.

No words can ever truly express my gratitude, but I will attempt to paint a vivid picture of my appreciation of his love, which I see every time he looks at me. When he walks into a room I instantly feel his protection, and the phrase that is spoken in silence is "I got you." His desire to make me happy—and his being man enough to ask God daily how to do handle the task—is what attracts me the most. I love the way he looks for me when I'm not in his sight, and once he lays his eyes and his heart upon me, he communicates that I'm his angel, his reason, and the only love that penetrates his soul. He loves me past my pain and straight to the joy of my destiny every single day. He is my blessing! I know that both my biological father and my heavenly father would echo the statement that "he is the truth." He stands with me in the storm, and then he ushers in the sunshine and a new beginning. When we met, I literally looked up and he was there, and in that moment he put his arms around my heart, which now beats with true love. I never knew a love like this before.

> Find a guy who calls you beautiful instead of hot, who calls you back when you hang up on him, who will lie under the stars and listen to your heartbeat, or will stay awake just to watch you sleep ... Wait for the boy who kisses your forehead, who wants to show you off to the world when you are in sweats, who holds your hand in front

of his friends, who thinks you're just as pretty without makeup on. One who is constantly reminding you of how much he cares and how lucky he is to have you ... The one who turns to his friends and says, "that's her."

—Harry Tottszer

The biggest transformation for me is that I now know that just because someone loves you, it doesn't meant that you have to get married or that the relationship is meant to be more than a season in your life. It may just be what it is—and that is love—and what is better than to have experienced love in the moment and to have been fully present within it? Love teaches you a more powerful lesson than any other act. It is there through breakup, breakdown, breakthrough, and breakout. It is truly a full-circle journey.

This is what transformation feels like!

E-V-O-L-ve: It's Time to Embrace the Foundation of Love

One of the most powerful moments of my transformation was when the word *evolve* took on a whole new meaning. I looked at the word *evolve,* and I heard a sweet, peaceful voice say, "Look closely." When I looked, the same gentle voice said, "Look at the first four letters spelled backward." I immediately started to write on the back of an envelope, because that was what I had to write on at the moment. If you haven't figured it out by now, those letters spell *love.*

Love and evolution go hand in hand. According to the Free Dictionary, the word *evolve* means to develop or achieve gradually; to work (something) out; to devise. The word *love* has several meanings, but the one that has always stood out for me as the foundation to follow is from 1 Corinthians 13:1–13. My favorite part is the statement, "Love is patient, love is kind. It does not envy, it does not boast, it is not proud. It does not dishonor others, it is not self-seeking, it is not easily angered, and it keeps no record of wrongs. Love does not delight in evil but rejoices with the truth. It always protects, always trusts, always hopes, and always perseveres. Love never fails."

In order to achieve true love, you need to grow gradually through different phases or journeys in life. You need time to work some things out and to work some things in. Once you are on the road of evolving, you will be able to settle in with the changes that are happening in your life. You will make peace with the fact that the change is in you rather than in the circumstance. Evolving is about *you*, not anyone else. It's about your growth, your journey, and the work that has to be done to achieve your true essence of love.

I'm sure you are familiar with the expression, "You have to love yourself before you can love somebody else"—it couldn't be truer. The transformation phases in your life will always be connected to evolving in some form. The journey that has helped you become comfortable in loving yourself has also set the foundation for you to give love in a healthy way. I remember wondering how I could expect any of my relationships to work when I wasn't healthy or whole. Even if the other person was healthy and whole, the minute I stepped in, the wholeness was compromised. One healthy plus one unhealthy adds up to an unhealthy relationship. When I realized this, a transformation took place in my mind.

Steps to Transformation

When I am speaking about transformation, people always ask what steps I took to achieve a positive personal transformation. My response is that the steps will be slightly different for everyone, and the order in which they happen may be different. For the most part, however, the steps of true transformation are very similar for all:

1. Be quiet so you can hear your inner voice.

Being alone and meditating is the most challenging step toward positive transformation. It involves shutting all the distractions down. It requires you to face and welcome both self-evaluation and evaluation of the things and people around you. This is your moment to let go of everything that is bothering you or hindering you and to get down to the roots of the issues. This is the most powerful moment of submitting to direction. This

is when you will meet peace and walk with it hand in hand on the road of restoration and truth.

2. Forgive the past.

If you are anything like me, you may be tempted to skip this step in the beginning of your transformation. I felt that this step stripped me down. I had no more pride left once I submitted fully to this process. I found that I was able to forgive everyone fully—except two people. I could have moved on to later steps, but until I'd completed the second step, I wouldn't have had a full transformation. Because of the two people I couldn't forgive fully, I had to come right back to that step and complete it before I was totally transformed.

3. Put on positive qualities; put away negative qualities.

Compare taking on qualities to putting on your clothes. Put on positive qualities daily, and put away negative qualities. The moment the negative thoughts come into your mind, put them away like a piece of clothing that is so itchy or uncomfortable that it affects your attitude whenever you wear it. That's how negative qualities feel: they affect your total attitude and the way you react. When you are positive, you feel good, productive, giving, and free. What you put in is what comes out!

4. Surround yourself with honest support.

You do not need an entourage. Your support right now may consist of just one person who can be honest and positive in your life—but one is all you need! True support is honest, and love is always honest. Your support person or people will be your cheerleaders for what is right and what is positive. They will hold you accountable to the commitments that you have made. You will know who these individuals are because they will always be aligned with positive energy and will always denounce negativity.

5. Be open to the possibility of the impossible.

When your heart opens up, the possibilities will too. Your heart has to open up in order to begin the first step of transformation. Once you begin to put on positivity and walk within it every day, you heart will begin to open up to even more possibilities. Once you become fully open to the impossible being possible, you are prepared to be totally comfortable in your transformation. The statements "I can't" or "It will never happen for me" will no longer exist in your life. Within this process, failure is no longer an option.

6. Be patient; change takes time.

I have always been in a rush for everything. I used to hate to go through the process of anything. I always wanted to just get to the bottom line and move on to the next project. Life and relationships were nothing but projects to me. But now I know that relationships have to be nurtured and maintained as you work on and through them. It takes commitment, goals, trust, and some degree of love to be fully present within a relationship during the process. My mother used to say, "It didn't take ten minutes for you to become the person you are now, so it's not going to take you ten minutes to transform a lifetime of character flaws." I had to learn what patience was, and I found that patience was all about me. I had failed in so many areas in my life because I was too fearful or lazy to go through the process.

If you allow the process to run its course, you will learn everything that the universe is trying to teach you. If you skip steps, the process will be incomplete, and therefore your steps and direction will be, too. Be patient, and reach your full potential.

Chapter 8

The Gift of Giving

Do you know what the gift of giving is? By the end of this chapter, you will. My personal journey in an unwanted relationship with cancer could inspire you and push you into doing something big. Determination, patience, motivation, strength, and courage will resound throughout this section.

The desire to give has always been one of my innate qualities. For as long as I can remember, the joy that I would feel when I gave was unlike any other pleasure. The smile that would appear when I gave a token of love, no matter how big or small, would satisfy my soul. It truly was intoxicating and addictive. Giving became a part of my life; I didn't reserve it for special occasions. It was a lifestyle.

In 2004 I moved to Washington DC. Little did I know that this move would set the foundation of my life for the next six years. It all started at a time in my life when I was holding a prestigious position as assistant dean of a university in California. I was told that no African American woman had held this position at this particular university. What an honor it was! I was thirty-two years old and thought I was on my way to a great career. I was a single mother; I had moved to Newport Beach, California; and life was good. I was recovering from a divorce and was feeling like the best revenge would be to succeed, and that is what I was on the path to doing. Then—*bam!*—in the middle of the bliss, it happened: I was pushed to the breaking point! My life was truly turned upside down.

The Diagnosis

I had been visiting the doctor for two years due to female problems, and after many visits, during which I had been checked for every STD under the sun, with repeated negative results, I was tired and embarrassed. My Pap smear kept coming back normal, but I knew something was wrong. One day I was in so much discomfort that I headed to the doctor on my lunch break. Usually I worked through lunch or had it in my office, but this day my spirit was crying out that something was wrong.

I arrived at the doctor's office and demanded a biopsy. I was frustrated and just wanted to know that I wasn't crazy. The doctor's response was essentially a suggestion that I speak to a therapist, because two years' worth of tests had been negative. I took control of the situation and again demanded the biopsy. The doctor agreed and performed the biopsy. Hurting and bleeding, I drove back to work and sat at my desk as if nothing had happened.

A couple of days later, my physician informed me that I had VIN III and possibly CIN III, and then I heard it could be cancer! *Okay, stop right there,* I thought. *What are you talking about? What are VIN III and CIN III?* I later learned that cervical intraepithelial neoplasia (CIN) is a severe type of dysplasia, or abnormal cell growth; in stage III the abnormal cells can be found in more than two-thirds of the lining of the cervix. Vulvar intraepithelial neoplasia (VIN) is the presence of abnormal cells in the skin of the vulva. Instead of an answer, the doctor gave me another diagnosis: most likely I had HPV. "Well, aren't you going to explain what that is?" I asked. The physician responded that I should research it over the weekend, because it was Friday, and it was time to leave the office.

I was an emotional wreck! I felt abandoned and helpless. Fear gripped my heart, and my body felt numb. But when my back is up against a wall, I come out swinging. And I began to feel that I was in a fight for my life.

I went to the library and found all the information that I could about human papillomavirus (HPV), a virus that affects both females and males. In 2004, the information about HPV was very inconsistent. It seemed that different sources all had different information regarding risks, prevention, and even the virus's very definition. There was only one common thread: HPV was an STD, or sexually transmitted disease.

How could I have contracted an STD? I was a good girl. My definition of a good girl was one who was not promiscuous. I was thirty-two and had had four sexual partners, two of whom were ex-husbands. How could I have an STD? After all, an STD was a nasty-girl disease. To my surprise, however, I learned that this was not a nasty little STD. To set the record straight, I will give you the true facts about HPV.

What Is HPV?

HPV is a member of the papillomavirus family of viruses that are capable of infecting humans. Like all papillomaviruses, HPV establishes productive infections only in the stratified epithelium of the skin or the mucous membranes. Stratified epithelium means closely packed sheets of epithelial cells arranged in layers over the external surface of the body and lining most of the hollow structures. The layers may include stratified squamous, stratified columnar, or stratified columnar ciliated types of cells. There are various subtypes of stratified epithelium, named for the type of cells on the surface. While the majority of the nearly two hundred known types of HPV cause no symptoms in most people, some types can cause warts, while others can, in a minority of cases, lead to cancers of the cervix, vulva, vagina, and anus in women or cancers of the anus and penis in men.

About forty types of HPV are typically transmitted through sexual contact, and they infect the genital region. Some sexually transmitted HPV types can cause genital warts. Persistent infection with "high-risk" HPV types—different from the ones that cause skin warts—may progress to precancerous lesions and invasive cancer. HPV infection is the cause of nearly all cases of cervical cancer; however, most infections of these types do not cause disease.

I have provided resources at the end of the chapter, and I strongly encourage you to learn more about HPV. After what I have been through, I feel it's my obligation to spread awareness to everyone I come into contact with. The good news is that if HPV or cervical cancer is detected early, there is a good chance that it is treatable. On the other hand, I have felt great sadness for women from low-income areas, as they are more likely to die of cervical cancer due to lack of education and lack of insurance.

I was in the small percentage of HPV cases that came with symptoms, such as itching and inflammation. Every time I went to the doctor I was treated for a yeast infection, a bladder infection, or an allergic reaction. The great irony is that they would test me for every possible STD *except* HPV.

The Move

Within a couple of weeks, I had a procedure due to the HPV, CIN III, and VIN III diagnoses. The procedure was a surgical excision that left me feeling as if I didn't understand what had happened. I was in pain and slipping into a depression. My body was in pain and inflamed, and I did not feel the same. I began to reflect on the future and decided that I wanted to make my life count. I was in a scary place. I had a vision of starting a foundation in Washington DC. Why DC? Well, besides the fact that I was receiving a divine direction from the most high, I knew Washington was the place where laws were created and there was great possibility for change. This was our nation's capital. The only problem was, how would I survive there? How would I start a foundation when I didn't have the first clue about starting one? How would I raise my baby, who was six at the time, in an unfamiliar place? Where would I go to continue treatment for an illness I didn't understand?

I didn't tell anyone the details of what I was thinking. I did know that if I was going to move to DC, I had to confirm employment. After extensive research, I found a job fit. I caught a flight to Washington, walked into the office of a director, and explained my plans and how I could be an asset to the company. I was told at the time that the individual who interviewed me felt I had the potential to grow quickly with the company and to become a campus director. However, all I wanted was a nonmanagement position with low stress, enough flexibility to take care of my health, and time to create my foundation. My interviewer informed me that he would not be making the final decision, but he set up an interview for the day before I was to return to California. That interview resulted in an educational liaison position that was less stressful for me. I received the job I wanted four weeks after the interview.

I had every intention of selling my expensive belongings, but because this transition was moving so fast, I ended up giving them all away to a family that didn't even have a bed. They had been sleeping on the floor with a brand-new baby. When you are have a destiny to fulfill and you have received divine orders, material things don't matter; as a matter of fact, nothing really matters except for completing your mission.

I told nearby friends and family about my plans, and their response was, "You are crazy!" As usual, when I did something that my mother didn't agree with, she ceased all communication with me. I needed support, but I knew that I wouldn't get it from her, so I pressed forward. When people don't understand your decisions that go against the norm, they will usually consider those decisions crazy. But some of the words associated with *crazy* are *passionate, wild, extreme,* and *indifferent.* Barack Obama is passionate, Oprah Winfrey has an extreme work ethic, and then you have Michelle Hannah, who is passionate and has embraced her purpose. Not bad for "crazy" …

Was this a crazy move? Yes! However, if you speak to anyone who has been successful, he or she will tell you that taking these kinds of risks is normal. I *did* lose my ordinary mind—but I traded it in for an extraordinary one.

One thing my mother made very clear was that I shouldn't take my daughter, because it would be hard enough for me to start a new life, deal with my health, and attempt to start a foundation. I agreed that she would stay in California for six months with my mother and then move to DC—not because my mother had made that statement but because I knew that it was in my daughter's best interest to stay in a healthy environment while I created stability in Washington. But I have to say that the hardest thing about this move was leaving my baby. We had never been separated, and she was the one thing that made all my mistakes seem less like great faults and more like life's greatest lessons and blessings. To this day I can't tell you what got me on that plane; the only explanation is that God was working behind the scenes.

New Life in DC

I arrived in Washington, and the moment I stepped off the plane I felt as though I had made a terrible mistake. Fear reintroduced itself, and I felt as though I couldn't pick up my luggage; I had no strength. As I stood there, my new employer called me on my cell phone and said they needed me to come in early. "Early" meant within two days instead of in two weeks. I didn't even know how to catch the Metro to the office where I was scheduled to report!

The promise that my supervisor would train me and get me acquainted with the area was suddenly null and void. Why? Well, I was told she was going through chemotherapy for ovarian cancer. *How ironic is that?* I thought. Needless to say, I had to suck up my tears and fears and quickly learn to maneuver around DC, Virginia, and Maryland. It was essential to my position that I know the market. If you have ever made a transition from the West Coast to the East Coast, you'll know it's a big one. The environment, the people, and all of the one-way streets were enough in themselves to make me consider packing my bags every week. Once I was settled in, six months later, the pain of my daughter's absence was so heavy on my heart that even now tears will fall when I think about that time.

In the first month I found a doctor, and that is an amazing story in itself. I had prayed and asked God to lead me to the right doctor, and as I sat there, overwhelmed by all the doctors listed on the Internet, one particular office jumped off the screen. I called and spoke to a nurse to whom I am forever grateful because she was so patient and she listened to my request. I requested that she refer me to a caring doctor who would be nice to me. I had had my share of no-bedside-manner, cold, insensitive physicians. She recommended a doctor who was exactly what I needed at the time. He diagnosed me with carcinoma in situ, which meant that the tumor had not spread to surrounding tissue. I went through another procedure and was given some medications that made me wish I were dead some days. In spite of it all, I made it through.

The Vision

In the midst of the many changes happening during my first six months in DC, I managed to write the plan for my foundation, and I met a strategic planner who was drawn to it. The resulting friendship assisted in the launch of the website, in a financial investment, in the development of templates for grant proposals, and in my getting the marketing expertise that I needed. We were now three committed, unpaid people, we worked hard toward the launch of Celebrate Life Foundation (CLF). Celebrate Life Foundation's mission is to educate, communicate, and promote the prevention of the sexually transmitted disease HPV, which can cause cervical cancer.

Many nights I didn't sleep. Some nights I was so focused that the only sign of the next day was the rising sun. This is what happens when you fully believe in what you are doing. Although we were clear regarding our mission at the time, the mission changed as we grew and learned more about the nonprofit industry. In 2005 we launched Celebrate Life Foundation, and it was an amazing night! We were so excited about the cancer survivors, the organization executives, and the health-care professionals who attended. Prior to the launch, we put together a documentary film titled *A Journey of Miracles*. The film's purpose was to highlight the stories of low-income women with cervical cancer. We specifically focused on giving these women a voice to express their unique journey and the challenges of not having healthcare. Looking back on it, I don't know how we did that within three weeks—unless it was that supernatural power! The documentary was a hit.

The launch was also a coming-out event for me because prior to that night I had spoken in the third person about a lady who had inspired me to create the foundation. Well, that night everyone found out that the lady was me. I have to tell you that when you decide to tell the truth about who you are, and you no longer need the approval of others, freedom is right around the corner.

For the six years that I lived in DC, I accomplished many things that I am proud of. Here are some of those accomplishments:

- Received my MBA with a minor in marketing

- Started a foundation

- Worked with many major pharmaceutical companies on advocacy for cervical cancer

- Participated in the major campaign for Gardasil, an HPV vaccination

- testified on Capitol Hill and at public hearings in other states about the need of HPV education

- gave several media interviews regarding HPV education

- created the first Survivor Pageant

- organized several conferences, seminars, webinars, and training sessions

- created educational manuals regarding health and HPV

- assisted many women to purchase medication and resources

- specifically worked with low-income women and teenagers

- partnered with other cancer organizations to promote HPV and cervical cancer education

- honored several people who might have gone unnoticed within the community and nonprofit industry

- through the Survivor Pageant, gave women an opportunity to feel empowered and to shine—not only low-income women, but also politicians, physicians, and other professionals who had suffered from some type of cancer

- produced a documentary on HPV

We have accomplished so much in the small amount of time that the organization has been in existence. The point is that Celebrate Life Foundation is *committed.* Our board of directors grew to include physicians, nurses, lawyers, and ordinary people who had a special gift for giving. The three original personnel turned into twelve, and our two partners turned into more than twenty organizations. As of today, the foundation's mission has changed again, and we have downsized to focus on two specific programs: the Survivor/Mending Heart Retreat and the CLF Stomp Out Cancer.

What Is a Survivor Pageant/Mending Heart Retreat?

Before I introduce the Survivor Pageant and Mending Heart Retreat, I must tell you how it all came about. While I was doing a radio interview, I had an "aha" moment. I started to think back to how I'd felt when I was diagnosed with carcinoma in situ of the cervix. My self-esteem had been very low, and I could barely look at myself in the mirror. I'd felt so unattractive, and the various medications I'd been on had caused reactions that were both internal and external. I thought about how much information and resources I'd used to research my own condition—if only I could have had someone to *educate* me about those resources. For instance, there was an overwhelming amount of information about cancer insurance.

I remember being stressed and scared and at times just wanted to be pampered. Unfortunately, there was no one to educate me at that time. I remember saying that one day I would like to have a pajama party and just let go as if I were fifteen years old. I would have loved to address all these issues in one weekend, or at least create a creative platform for cancer survivors to vent, learn, teach, grow, and experience living in the moment. If I found a way to do this, I felt, I would succeed in giving a great gift. In the next moment, I was writing a plan for what I called a Survivor Pageant/ Mending Heart Retreat for cancer survivors.

A Mending Heart Retreat supports cancer survivors and patients with HPV, VIN III, CIN III, cervical cancer, or other female-related cancers. Participants attend an off-site location for a three-day period in a seminar setting. The seminars address not only health-fitness initiatives but also life-fitness initiatives, such as financial management, self-improvement, annual screenings, stress management, and sociological enhancement. In addition to the seminars, the ladies attend a pajama party that focuses on skin care and living in the moment. The main goal is to provide underserved women who are battling cancer with education about their disease and other health-related issues, to provide resources for affordable medicine, and to financially assist women to be vaccinated if there is a need. Research representatives, cancer survivors, guest speakers and facilitators, and doctors are among the staff attendees. The conference culminates in a Survivor Pageant.

To survive means to stay alive, to live, and to live *on*. It is truly special to be a cancer survivor. It is important for women to have a forum that encourages them not to be afraid to tell the tale. A Survivor Pageant is a proprietary celebration designed by CLF to recognize cancer survivors through a series of events. The celebration is used not only for entertainment purposes but also as a creative learning platform to promote HPV awareness, new vaccines, and other health-related resources. Participants are selected from local hospitals, support groups, churches, sororities, and by referrals. The audience consists of contestants' family members, health-care professionals, directors and employees from support groups, political figures, and church groups. One of the event's most important goals is to educate people of all ages in a creative learning environment. The pageant winner, crowned Ms. CLF of the targeted state, receives many prizes from our sponsors and represents CLF in reaching out to her community. The runners-up are also involved in voluntary outreach programs designed by CLF.

Since its conception, we have had six Survivor Pageants and Mending Heart Retreats. We have successfully reached thousands of women with this initiative, and we look forward to hosting many more retreats in the future.

The Gift of Giving: Survivor Stories

I have met many women who are survivors in one way or another. However, there are some stories that have specifically touched me, and I'm sure they will touch you in a special way, too. For the sake of protecting the innocent, I will use fictitious names.

I met BJ when my foundation was just finding its voice in the community. I wanted to put together a documentary that educated people about HPV, and how it relates to cervical cancer, through the voices of women from low-income areas. I found two women who would stand up, and one of them will be forever etched in my heart. BJ had seven children, and she loved them with a rare intensity. BJ was thirty-two at the time, and she had gone through many surgeries for her cervical cancer. She ended up suffering other health problems due to the surgeries and cancer. When I met her, however, she had a big smile.

To help you understand the full picture, I'll tell you that I was from a middle-class household, and I had never seen what "project" living was like. I wasn't used to the roaches and mice that existed in these low-income housing projects. However, when I walked into BJ's one-bedroom apartment, the roaches and the mice couldn't overshadow her big smile. Her willingness to share her journey and her amazing story was humbling. In that moment, I knew that BJ and I would be connected.

I ended up mentoring BJ, and she moved from the projects to a nice apartment. I gave her a suit that she was convinced clinched her being offered an assistant manager position. The backstory about the suit is funny. I had intended to give BJ a fuchsia suit that I had only worn once. I had another suit that I had just bought from Saks Fifth Avenue. Well, a male cousin of mine just heard me say, "Give her the suit." He didn't hear me specify the fuchsia suit. So, of course, he gave her the new suit that I had spent my last five hundred dollars on. My first reaction was to strangle him, but then I thought, *It's just a suit.* I wanted BJ to look her best—and she did. At that moment, the opportunity to give was priceless.

BJ was in one of our first Survivor Pageants. She shared with me that she had never been in a hotel room like the one she was staying in for the weekend. A year later she was stricken with cancer yet again, and this time it was terminal. I didn't understand. We were the same age, and her life had changed for the better. Why was she dying now? I had gone on vacation for three days because I hadn't given myself a break since creating the foundation. As soon as I made it to Florida, however, I received a call that BJ was not going to make it. Heartbroken, I immediately flew back.

The emotions we both felt are impossible to put into words. But I was gratified when BJ told me that my foundation had helped her to live in the moment and that she finally understood what it was to be a phenomenal woman. She expressed that she wasn't scared to die anymore because she felt that she had celebrated her life. She thanked me and told me she loved me, and shortly after that she passed away. I spoke at BJ's funeral, but I tell you, you are never prepared to say good-bye to a friend—especially one who is only thirty-six. The gift she gave to me was the understanding of the phrase "Judge not, lest ye be judged."

Amantha's amazing story always seems to come to mind when I am having a short pity party. Once I think about her courage, I immediately leave the party. Amantha was in our second Survivor Pageant. She reluctantly accepted the invitation, and I'm so glad she did. Amantha was a nurse who was diagnosed with breast cancer. Her husband supported her through her journey—he was truly the love of her life—but suddenly he died. As if that weren't enough, her daughter was then diagnosed with breast cancer in the same breast as Amantha's. Amantha supported her daughter and was there for her every step of the way. Sadly, her daughter lost the battle with breast cancer. Amantha had lost the love of her life *and* her only daughter. She was devastated and empty, but as a nurse, she continued to help others. She moved past her pain every day and saw the need to ease others' pain.

I connected with Amantha's story from the very beginning. She won that Survivor Pageant, and in that moment she realized why I had been so persistent with her. She realized how her story had changed the lives of so many women in that audience. A couple of years later she spoke at another

Survivor Pageant and stated that I had saved her life. I was so humbled, because she had changed my life and allowed me to celebrate hers; there was no way I felt that I had saved her life. She further explained that what she felt I did for her that weekend was to give her the gift of hope and the will to celebrate her life every day. After all, she had survived! The gift she gave to me was the knowledge that there is joy past the deepest pain.

JC will always be an amazing woman. I knew JC for a very short period of time. What a woman she was! She was vivacious and one of the most helpful people I have ever met. JC was a fighter. She had lost her husband, gone through several surgeries, and survived cancer. Her children thought the world of her, and she volunteered her time to help many women overcome their fears. Many times she would sit with women while they went through chemo or needed her support at the doctor's office. JC was simply selfless. Her help was critical to me in putting together the Survivor Pageants. Due to a rough turn in her health, she was unable to participate in one of the Survivor Pageants, but she kept her door open and let our organization know that she was only a call away.

I was moved to honor JC at that Survivor Pageant, and I am so glad I did. She looked beautiful on that day. She beamed as she accepted her awards. Her children and family presented her with love, hugs, and flowers. They were so proud of their mother. So many people spoke about how JC had changed their lives and eased their pain. That was on a Saturday. JC fell sick on that Monday, and on Wednesday she was in a coma. She never came out of the coma. The gift she gave me was the insight to never take a moment for granted. Honestly, this is the greatest of all gifts I have received.

A New Direction to Giving

Due to the recession that started in 2007, grants and personal donations were slowing down, but we were still providing programs that I believe truly made a difference. At this point the Survivor Pageants were booming, and we were working diligently with the American Cancer Society. We had quite a buzz in the DC metropolitan area. My speaking platform was growing, and I was convinced that my voice was a powerful tool.

At this point in life I truly understood what giving was all about. Between 2005 and 2008, the foundation gave so much from a philanthropic point of view that it was difficult to imagine not being able to give at that level in 2009. Then, in November 2008, I was laid off from the job I had had since I'd arrived in DC in 2004. I began to feel just a little bit of the recession, but I had some savings and severance pay. I took about three months off to refocus, and by January 1, 2009, I was offered another position that seemed to be a better fit than my previous one. In 2009, I had to reorganize the foundation. This resulted in a new mission and a new way of thinking about giving. We had to be smarter and more selective in where we directed our support, as our budget had been reduced significantly.

For me, giving continued to be addictive. Although I didn't have nearly as much money to give, I so desperately wanted to help people who were less fortunate, and to educate people, that I used my own money plenty of times. I realized I couldn't make a habit of this when my credit cards reached the limit. It was at that moment that I realized I was totally comfortable giving because it somewhat prevented me from focusing on my own issues. The truth is, my self-worth was very low, and I felt that everyone else was more important than I was. I didn't feel I was worthy of receiving love. I could give the gift, but I couldn't receive it.

Then—*bam!*—in 2010, I became ill once again. This time it wiped me out physically and mentally, and I truly came to understand the meaning of giving. I realized I first had to give to *myself* everything that I had been giving to others. I had to pamper myself and make myself feel special, just as I had done so many times for other women. I had to teach myself about positive thinking, loving myself, and being accountable for my health—just as I had taught others for the last six years.

You cannot define the gift of giving until you understand first what it is to give the biggest gift: love to yourself. Only then can you give fully. Another "aha" moment during my transformation—during the total renewal of my mind—happened in September 2010, after the Philadelphia Survivor Pageant. I began to feel that the three days of gift giving, seminars, pampering, sisterly love, and promises that the ladies made to themselves were just a temporary fix. Don't get me wrong—the pageant was an amazing time, and the survivors were over-the-top about the weekend, but I faced the reality that a weekend is just a weekend. I had started the foundation to change lives and to teach people how to live not just beyond cancer but in the moment. Making *every* moment count was essential to the commitment to *living*—not just surviving.

Living Your Best Life—Every Moment

How does one live in the moment? How could I teach these women in two to three days how to transform their thinking and to live their best lives? Because of my amazing journey, I have the great privilege of sharing with all of you my solution to these questions. And guess what? It works! What follows are the keys to living your best life—every moment.

1. Transform your thoughts: denounce the negative and confess the positive.

You must first get control of your mind, because if you are not careful, once you embrace one negative thought, another will follow, and before you know it, depression and low self-esteem will have set up camp. When a negative thought comes to mind, immediately tackle it with a positive thought.

2. Write down your plan of action.

When you write down a plan of action, you are committing to doing the work, and you are now accountable to the commitments you have made. You have to be very specific with this plan. It can't be vague. If your plan is to lose weight, then write down why you want to lose weight, how you are going to do it, and when you will make the time to exercise. Attach a number to your goal so that it will be measurable.

3. Tell someone who is supportive and who will hold you accountable.

Find a person who is supportive and trustworthy. This person should have your best interest at heart. Ask him or her to commit to your mission because he or she wants to see you succeed. For example, if you are looking to lose weight, this person will motivate you to make healthier choices when all you want is cupcakes.

4. Take as many love breaks as you need for yourself.

Don't wait for anyone to give you what you need and deserve. If your favorite flowers are gardenias, go and get some. If you want to be romanced, who knows better than you what you need in order to feel romanced? Go and savor your favorite meal while enjoying a great view. Listen to your favorite song and sing at the top of your voice, or dance as if you don't care that people are watching. This is your love break. Once you have conquered taking a break to love yourself, then you can share these breaks with others.

5. Practice gratitude.

Life is the greatest gift you have—be grateful for it. We all have issues or circumstances that we wish we could change in an instant, but that should not prevent us from showing gratitude. Gratitude is so powerful because it helps you to focus on the gifts, blessings, and talents that help us succeed in this world. When you show gratitude, it'll come right back at you, and that will result in positive emotions. It's a win-win situation!

6. Practice the gift of giving.

Whether it's donating your time or money to your favorite foundation or just complimenting a stranger, always be aware of the world around you. If you want to change the world, change yourself first, and through your transformation, the world will change around you. Volunteering your time may seem small, but trust me, organizations will appreciate your help. You will be making a difference in someone's day, which is making a difference in that person's life. When I am having a bad-hair day and someone I don't know spontaneously says that my hair is beautiful, I instantly feel better.

Spontaneous acts of kindness are unexpected, and you can't be sensitive to those moments unless you are making them happen yourself.

7. Practice total forgiveness.

Forgiveness is the greatest gift you can give yourself besides love. It is a decision to let go of resentment and thoughts of revenge. The act that hurt or offended you may always remain a part of your life, but forgiveness can lessen its grip on you and help you focus on other, positive parts of your life. Letting go of grudges and bitterness makes way for compassion, kindness, and peace—even toward the person who hurt you.

Forgiveness can lead to the following:

- healthier relationships
- greater spiritual and psychological well-being
- less stress and hostility
- lower blood pressure
- fewer symptoms of depression, anxiety, and chronic pain
- lower risk of alcohol and substance abuse

8. Smile! Smile! Smile!

Smiling is true medicine to the soul. As I started to smile more and cry less, the windows of joy opened up. I suggest that the first thing you should do when you wake up is smile. This will set the tone for your day. Before you give in to stress, anger, or frustration, take a moment and smile. I know this can be hard, but remember: you make the choice not to smile, but that only makes your situation worse. I understand that there is a time for your expressions to be serious, but if you could focus on wearing a smile on your face and in your heart for 80 percent of the day, you would not only be blessed but also be a blessing to others. Have you ever noticed that when you say the word *smile*, your mouth automatically starts to move into a smile?

Now, embrace your journey, and enjoy each and every moment of it!

* * *

At this point in life, we are reorganizing CLF, rebuilding and embracing growth. My daughter and I have been reunited on a daily basis for two years now, and we are doing well. Although it was challenging during the six-year period when she was visiting me in DC and I was catching flights back and forth from coast to coast, our bond never was broken. It worked at the time, though I would be dishonest if I didn't say that I regretted the setup at times. I realized that, regardless of the relationship between me and my mom, she was the best grandmother that she could be. I am thankful that my daughter was able to experience that.

I realize that I helped many people during that six-year period, but I've had to forgive myself for missing some precious moments that I will never get back with my daughter. I've also had to forgive myself for wanting to continue to please my mother by allowing my child to stay in California. I am so glad that I finally took control of my life and took my power back. I live in the moment, and I embrace all the special moments that my daughter and I experience daily. Overall, I'm SMILING!

Resources on HPV

- www.hpvinfo.com
- www.cdc.gov/hpv
- www.hpv.com

Chapter 9

Living beyond All the Broken Pieces

"Living beyond the Broken Pieces" is a summation of all the phases that will lead you back full circle in the most important areas of your life. Seeing my life journeys, you will realize how to live every day beyond all the fear, pain, brokenness, and disappointment. Through every obstacle, you will take a journey that addresses common issues and their outcomes. This chapter sums up the statement "When God fixes it, it's as if it never happened!"

On December 9, 2010, I watched Oprah Winfrey on a Barbara Walters special, and I was so inspired! Oprah has been an unbelievable influence in my life. On the show, she stated that she would tell God to use her till he used her up, as in the old Bill Withers song, "Use Me." To be used by anyone other than God is a prerequisite to brokenness, but when God is using you, it results in *life* beyond the brokenness. I was touched and moved to tears—and then to sobbing. As I got myself together, the words of a classic Harry Nilsson song came to my mind: "I Can't Live if Living Is without You." At that moment the full circle made so much sense, and I was arrested by an overwhelming desire to write.

A Full-Circle Journey

In 2009 I became familiar with the phrase "full circle." Full circle means coming back to your starting point and turning your life around completely.

In doing this, you create conscious choices and live a deliberate life. I began to find this phrase in the most unexpected places; it would be staring me in the face. I wouldn't be looking for it—it would just be there. One day, at my grandmother's house, I was reading a plaque on the wall, and to my surprise, again I saw the phrase "full circle." I knew that the universe was trying to tell me something. What that something was, I had no clue.

Isn't it funny how, when we are not ready to let go, the past comes up in every area of our lives? When we decide to "let go and let God," we can finally relax in the moment, get out of our own way, and receive the blessings and lessons.

Full Circle with Health

My illness turned around full circle. According to some physicians, my health was in the worst shape in 2010, and there was nothing I could do about it. But I truly believe that it was through God, positive thinking, forgiveness, and the release of pain that my body started to heal itself. In 1995, a doctor told me that I needed to change my diet and implement regular exercise in my life. He stated that my problems were related to my poor diet and lack of exercise. I didn't obey, and the consequence was that my body suffered. I was in severe pain, in and out of the hospital, unable to walk or to feel my right leg, suffering from debilitating headaches, unable to keep my food down, and the list goes on ... I am convinced that the food I was putting into my body was a big part of my issues. Now I am finally doing the right thing: I have come full circle—to what I knew was right in the first place.

Full Circle with Relationships

A lifelong relationship taught me something about what it means to come full circle: the attributes that attracted you and disappointed you will still have the same effects if neither you nor your partner has gone through a transformation. The positive thing about this particular relationship was that it brought me back to the street where I had grown up. I had not been on that street since my dad died. I had been determined never to visit it, but now my relationship forced me to face my deepest pain. I hadn't been able to ride through the streets of my hometown, but again, I finally had to face it now. While conquering my fears and pain, I realized I had some healing and forgiving to do. I understood that I had been brought back to where I'd begun so that I could finally heal and move forward. It was another case of coming full circle.

My most painful separation was the one between my mother and me. When I came back to California, I thought the close relationship we used to have would become even closer. Then I realized that when I had moved to DC, I had grown up and transformed—but my mother rejected that transformation. She rejected it because I was no longer the person she thought I was or wanted me to be. In my opinion, my mother was very controlling. I tried to do most of the things she said, but because her journey wasn't my journey, I was often resentful, hurt, and angry. I would compare it to living a very uncomfortable lie. Any lie is uncomfortable because it forces you to be something you are not, which in turn creates pressure. Eventually, the more determinedly my mother would push, the more I would do the opposite of what she wanted.

When I was a kid, if my mother told me that I didn't like a certain food, I wouldn't eat it. If she said that I wouldn't like traveling out of the country, I would take it as gospel. But years later, I discovered that the way she viewed relationships was very different from the way I had learned to experience healthy relationships. I wanted my child to eat healthfully, but my mom felt that healthy food was tasteless and her grandchild should be able to have fried and well-seasoned food. Usually foods that are highly seasoned are high in sodium, and deep-fried foods contribute to obesity. I wanted to be different and to make different decisions for my child. My "aha" moment came when someone made me some grilled chicken with nothing but natural herbs—no salt—it was delicious and healthy!

Through the pain, frustration, and tug-of-war of this relationship, and after my breakdown, I decided I had to restructure my life. I had to make the hard decision of separating from my mother. I had to take control of my life and be comfortable with my own decisions, no matter what. I realized that the full circle was a transformation of myself so that I could forgive and heal. I take responsibility for not standing up for myself long ago—that was my fault. I can't change my mom, but I can change myself. After working through forgiveness, I now know that she never intended to hurt me or to cripple me as much as I allowed her to. I realize that, in her way of loving, she believed with all of her heart that most of the things she did were correct. Oftentimes it takes self-reflection and therapy to show us that we have handled a situation terribly wrongly. My relationship with my mother is a lifetime relationship that is in a seasonal phase. Our separation was just for that season, and I had a feeling that in the future I would meet up with my mother again on the road of restoration and redemption.

March 19, 2012, was the day we met on that road. Forgiveness was what led me to that road, and love was what motivated me to embrace restoration. It may be a long process of restoration, but after all, my relationship with my mother began with the conception of my birth. Now that's coming full circle.

Full Circle with Work

I recall that as a little girl I wanted to help people; I wanted to help heal the brokenhearted and give to all who were in need. I loved writing, but I suffered from dyslexia, so I didn't think that I would ever be a writer. I tried nursing, but I finally decided on a degree in psychology and a minor in sociology. Along the way, however, I saw there was a bigger financial return in the field of business, so I changed my course. Many years passed, and eventually I ended up in the education field. It was still not my calling, but at least I was helping people and using my voice through presentation. Then came the mission and vision of the Celebrate Life Foundation, and for the first time in my life I was alive and totally in my element. My story attracted speaking engagements, and the information I was presenting was life changing. I was still not ready to run to my destiny, however, so I played it safe and stayed in education.

When I moved back to California, my foundation work was on hold and my speaking engagements came to a halt. I was no longer completely happy in education, and I was very confused about my direction. I started to realize that when you are neither happy nor comfortable with yourself, everything around you begins to suffer. I still didn't want to use my voice. I was so unhappy about being in California and not in DC that I began to question whether I really believed in what I was communicating to others. Somewhere along the line I stopped focusing on helping people in education and concentrated more on the numbers associated with my performance review. After my last Survivor Pageant, I was empty and tired of feeling as if I had created only a temporary solution to a much greater problem.

Thank the Lord for full circle. It became very obvious why I had come full circle back to the place where I was born. There was so much I had to face and make peace with before I would be ready to embark on the greatest journey in my life. After my many breaking points—the breakup, breakdown, breakthrough, and breakout phases—I was completely ready to embrace my purpose. I was healthy on the inside, and my decisions were totally conscious. I was now living my best life, and professionally I was back on the speaking circuit with the right message—and I'm sure you figured out that I accepted my calling as an author.

Full Circle with Losing Weight

Losing weight was one of the hardest challenges for me, mainly because of a lack of discipline and commitment. I really wanted to lose ten pounds, but instead I gained ten pounds. After my metabolism slowed down, I wanted to lose fifteen, but instead I gained fifteen. It used to be that if I looked great in my clothes, then I was satisfied—but then I reached the breaking point, and I decided enough was enough. As I stood in front of the mirror, naked, I was repulsed and depressed. The truth was staring me in the face: my body was an imposter. I was screaming to get out, and that very day I began to commit my mind to the journey I knew I had to take.

I found a gym and committed to working out five days a week, no matter what. I increased veggies and fruit and decreased sugar by 80 percent, and over time I began to see a difference. It continues to be a daily struggle, but it is one that I conquer every day. My confidence is growing, and I'm feeling better both naked and clothed.

Again I've experienced the full-circle journey. I've returned to the starting point that encouraged a healthy diet and exercise—no more crash diets for me. My choice to change was strategic and deliberate. It did occur to me that this was the same information I had received over fifteen years ago—why couldn't I just have committed to it at that time? But then I let the past be the past and chose to live in the moment. This moment was one of triumph, and I wasn't about to allow "woulda, coulda, shoulda" to steal my moment.

Full Circle with My Daddy

Sixteen years ago my dad died. I thought it was the worst day that I would ever experience. Right before he died, my dad expressed his true desire for me—that I would stop worrying about what other people felt and said about me. He wanted me to make my own decisions and live for *me*. He explained that holding grudges only hurt *me*. The offending persons have gone on with their lives, he told me, and they are still in control of *your* life because you are giving them that power. Dad wanted me to experience what love truly is, but only when I had experienced life for myself and had taken the time to know myself. He wanted me to be free, and he wanted me to finally know that I was more than enough. Sixteen years later, all that he wanted for me has come full circle. The most profound triumph on this journey is that I know that I am more than enough!

Running Back to You

While going through many full-circle moments, I realized that the one who settled it for me was the true starting point. In realizing who that was—and who *I* was—I was moved to write this love letter:

I can't live if living is without you. I can't give if giving is without you. The full-circle journey has always been about you. I get it now—I CAN'T LIVE if it's without YOU! I can't live in the moment if YOU are not fully present. I can't exist without YOU. I can't breathe without YOU. I can't fulfill my purpose without YOU. Living is with YOU, in and all through me, and through everything I do. I can't take one more step without YOU. I can't write this book and live this journey without YOU. I can't forgive myself without YOU. I can't face the highest mountains without YOU. I can't live up to any titles without YOU. I can't be in this world without YOU. My smile isn't a genuine smile anymore, and I know why—it's because I need YOU to make it genuine. I need YOU to carry me right now. I need to feel safe, and for some reason I trust that YOU can do this. I never trusted YOU fully, but I feel that if I give YOU everything and lay every burden and care on YOU then YOU will carry this for me. YOU will carry me at this time when I can't carry myself. All that I hoped another human could be for me, YOU are. The need that has been in me since I was a little girl is a void that YOU are going to fill. I can feel it. My heart has always been empty regarding that space of safety, but I now know that unconditional love exists in YOU. At this moment, MY GOD, YOU love me just the way I am, which seems a MESS. Through breakup, breakdowns, breakthroughs, breakout, and complete transformation, YOU love me. My heart was broken, and YOU mended it; I know this.

The world has used me till it's used me up, so God, I trust you to use me, and I welcome you using me until you use me up. When I have your higher power leading me, the use of my talents and my life is genuine, innocent, and full of love. There's no more worrying about being taken advantage of, because when you lead me and I follow in

the footsteps of your higher power, nothing but greatness
will result.

After writing this, I was filled with inspiration and with hope. It hit me that
what I had written was a beautiful love letter to God. I truly understood
why I titled this book *The Breaking Point: A Full-Circle Journey*. It was the
breaking points that led me to change my entire life and motivated me to
make deliberate and conscious decisions. Living was no longer a strenuous
task; it was a privilege, a gift, and the best thing that could have happened
to me. I had to live beyond all the brokenness in order to be fully present
within my freedom and be who I was and who I desired to be.

Let Go and Let God

I have always heard that God might not come when you want him
but he is always on time. I wrote that love letter back in November of
2010, but let me tell you: when I least expected it, on the last day of
January, God spoke directly to my heart. I happened to be looking at
YouTube, and somehow I ended up viewing a tribute from Marvin Sapp
and his kids on the day of the funeral of MaLinda Sapp. He started to
sing the song "Let Go" (and Let God). This song had been a testimony
when he was watching his wife suffer from cancer. When he sang that,
everything in me began to heal. I then immediately went to the video by
DeWayne Woods so I could hear the whole song, and in that moment,
I let go. I let go of every pain, embarrassment, trial, hurt, impossibility,
insurmountable mountain, loss, struggle, and battle. I let go of every
hater, every unforgiveness, lie, worry, emptiness, lack of real love, and
everything that was broken. I let go and let God have his way. I stopped
worrying about how the story would end, and the moment I did that,
things literally started to happen—not the next day, not hours later, but
right at that moment. When God answers and speaks to your heart, he
can truly heal all that has caused you pain and has prevented you from
achieving true freedom.

In my new freedom, everything opened up. I received my second master's degree, was certified as a relationship and life coach, and started a new business (Mikel Life Coaching). All of this happened within a year, because when I embraced the steps of transformation and put them into motion, I attracted all that was meant for me. It didn't take a long time once I submitted.

How do you live beyond all the brokenness? You let go, and you let the peace and serenity shower you and motivate you to live your best life! That's all I would accept at that time in my life. There was no other option but to let go of what had happened in my past, to live in the moment, and to embrace whatever the future would hold. I knew that my future would include the most illuminating light that I would ever experience, mainly because my present was a reflection of what was to come.

Much love and support,

Michelle